Special Educati ɔok

The law on children with special needs

9th edition

Contents

© 2005 Published by the Advisory Centre for Education 1C Aberdeen Studios, 22 Highbury Grove, London N5 2DQ
www.ace-ed.org.uk September 2005
Revised by Margaret McGowan. Designed by Sally Doust. Printed by Nuffield Press Ltd., Abingdon, Oxfordshire
ISBN 1 870672 31 3

How to use this handbook

This handbook has been written for parents of children and young people who have special educational needs (SEN) and/or disabilities and those who advise and support them. It begins with a description of the legal framework which underpins the detailed practice which must be followed when a child with special educational needs is identified. It goes on to describe the way that maintained schools and local authorities should provide help for those children. Many will also be disabled children and the handbook now includes a chapter on disability rights and duties as they relate to education. A number of new summaries of cases on disability discrimination and special educational needs have been included to give a flavour of the decisions made by the courts. Please note, however, that these cannot always represent the full legal effect of each case, also new cases may change the law after the publication of this handbook. For this reason you should not rely on the summaries if you are planning legal action. If in doubt seek legal advice.

This handbook aims to explain the legal requirements and good practice in straightforward language so that parents know what to expect and what part they can play in securing the right help for their children. It describes the way that the school system is organised and explains who is responsible for what. It details the formal assessment process which usually leads to the making of a Statement of special educational needs. It also describes the system for appeals and claims to the Special Educational Needs and Disability Tribunal.

Understanding the system is one thing, knowing where you as a parent can be involved and take action is another. With that in mind the handbook gives practical step-by-step advice on getting extra help at School Action and School Action Plus, contributing to the assessment, analysing a draft statement and participating in the annual review. This advice, called Parents' Action, is found in sections at the end of Chapters 2 to 5.

Successful education is a partnership between home and school. We hope this handbook will help parents become confident partners, working with their schools and local authorities to get the best for their children.

Legal references

There are Acts of Parliament and Regulations which set out what schools and local authorities must do by law, and Codes of Practice and government guidance which advise schools and local authorities. All of them encourage close collaboration with parents.

This handbook covers the law on children with special educational needs in England and Wales, but not Scotland or Northern Ireland. Acts of Parliament are largely the same for England and Wales but guidance and regulations may differ. Currently these differences are small and where relevant we point them out in the text. References to the SEN Code also correspond in most cases; where they differ we give both references. Some guidance, notably the *SEN Toolkit* and *Inclusive Schooling* applies to England only. Similar guidance is available in Wales – in the *Handbook of Good Practice for Children with SEN* and *Inclusive Education*. Details of how to get guidance is found in further information at the end of this handbook.

In this handbook we use 'must' when the law says something has to happen and 'should' when the government expects something to happen.

In many places we print the relevant section or paragraph numbers of the law and guidance that is being described within the text. To save space this is done in a form of shorthand. For example **S316 EA96** means **Section 316** of the **Education Act 1996** and **COP 7.20** means **Chapter 7, paragraph 20** of the **SEN Code of Practice**. Case law references are generally to the Education Law Reports published by Jordans and are abbreviated to ELR.

Who does what?

The Department for Education and Skills (DfES) – the central government department responsible for education policy in England – is headed by a Secretary of State for Education who is an elected Member of Parliament (MP) appointed to the post by the Prime Minister. From time to time the DfES issues advice in the form of Codes of Practice or other guidance. In Wales these are issued by the Welsh Assembly Government (WAG) which also produces Regulations.

Children's services authority, Children's trust, local authority, local education authority (LEA) – these are all terms to describe the local body which, under the **Children Act 2004,** will be responsible for a range of local children's services including most schools. Children's trusts go beyond local authority departments by including children's health services. They may also include other services such as Connexions and Youth Offending Teams. Children's trusts will normally sit within the local authority and report to the Director of Children's Services who will report through the Chief Executive to elected councillors.

Terms such as 'children's trusts' and children's services are more likely to be used in place of the more familiar local education authority. In this guide we use the term local authority, except where we are quoting the legislation directly, in which case we would generally continue to use local education authority.

The governing body of a school is the body of people elected, appointed and co-opted to manage it. It must hold meetings at least once every term. The headteacher, who is appointed by the governing body, is responsible for the day to day running of the school.

The special educational needs co-ordinator (SENCO) is the member of school staff who has responsibility for the day-to-day management of the school SEN policy and co-ordination of provision for individual children.

Understanding the jargon

The world of education is full of jargon. You should always ask if you are not clear about the language that is being used. However, some words and acronyms are used so often it is worth getting to know them. The most common, used in this Special Education Handbook, are listed in the box below. Throughout the handbook we explain the meaning of certain words and jargon. Look for the magnifying glass symbol for definitions.

Advice	written reports from parents, teachers and other professionals on a pupil's special educational needs
COP	Code of Practice on Special Educational Needs
DDA	Disability Discrimination Act
DfES	Department for Education and Skills
WAG	Welsh Assembly Government
EA	Education Act
EP	Educational Psychologist
IEP	Individual Education Plan
LEA	Local Education Authority
LA	Local Authority
CSA	Children's Services Authority
PPO	Parent Partnership Officer
SEN	Special Educational Needs
SENCO	Special Educational Needs Co-ordinator
SENDA	Special Educational Needs and Disability Act 2001

Setting the scene

Where schools are properly supported by government policies, funding and proper training for staff, inclusion works.

This new edition of our handbook has been revised during a period of great debate in the field of special education. It is a debate fuelled in part by the recantation of the person whose report in 1978 led to the present system. Baroness Warnock, then Mary Warnock, took up both inclusion and parents' involvement as the two major themes of her report. More recently she seems to be wavering at least on inclusion and appears to have accepted the view that the system is too bureaucratic for parents.

ACE's view is that where schools are properly supported by government policies, funding and proper training for staff, inclusion works. The evidence of our exclusion advice lines tells us that the opposite is happening in some schools. Around three quarters of our callers on those lines have children with special educational needs. That said many schools do combine inclusion with achievement and reap the benefits of involving parents and valuing all children.

ACE strongly disagrees that the problem for parents is bureaucracy. Ever since the flawed Audit Commission report *Special Educational Needs – a mainstream issue* [2002], bureaucracy has been used by government as an excuse to reduce accountability to parents. For example, among all the documents which schools produce, the modest individual education plan (IEP) is continually being highlighted in attacks on red tape, yet it plays a useful role in making sure parents and children are involved in deciding targets and support and monitoring progress, particularly for those children without a Statement.

The parents ACE speaks to every day on our advice lines may be worn down with trying to get support for their child and do complain of bureaucracy. But they are not complaining that their child is being assessed or that the help is being written on a Statement or that they are asked to meetings to review an IEP. When you dig below the surface you discover that parents' complaints are largely about failures of the system rather than the system itself: backlogs in assessments, hold ups in getting provision, difficulties with school placements, and Statements which are unclear about the help which is to be provided.

In ACE's view the system itself, with its guiding principle of matching needs with help, could not be more compelling. The problem is that local authorities are having to square the circle between the law and local policies and funding. The law says that a child's education is so important that extra help to give them the same learning opportunities as other children must not be rationed, delayed or subject to blanket cuts. But where resources are not provided to match this legal duty, local authorities respond with policies which try to impose a form of rationing.

Government backed off reducing children's legal rights on Statements in 1998 when the outcry which followed the Green Paper's proposals on special education revealed the extent of parent hostility to a change in the law. Instead it has found a less direct way of reducing Statements and this, in ACE's view, threatens not only inclusion but works against the principles set out in the Green Paper, *Every Child Matters* [2003] of early intervention, preventative work and integrated services for children. The current policy is to encourage authorities to delegate nearly all the funds for special educational needs to schools. This is despite the recognition in *Removing Barriers to Achievement, the Government's Strategy for SEN* [2004] that the majority of local authorities have not yet developed adequate arrangements for monitoring outcomes for pupils with SEN especially in relation to delegated funding. The aim, according to the strategy, is to encourage early identification and inclusion; but again from ACE's experience on the advice lines we know that the opposite is often the case. For years schools have had budgets which are not earmarked to spend on children with SEN without Statements. The track record of meeting the needs of those children and accounting for that spending has not been impressive. There are many other demands on schools' budgets and the rewards for meeting the needs of children with special educational needs are limited to the personal satisfaction of individual teachers – there are no public league tables of schools who do well with this group.

For this reason ACE finds the extension of these funding arrangements to children with even greater needs very worrying. Schools often struggle to identify complex difficulties and the fact that many young people have behaviour problems which stem from undiagnosed special educational needs is well known.

To make matters worse, many local authorities are coupling delegation with a policy of no more Statements except for special school placements, leaving schools to decide whether to buy in expertise. Many schools do their best but SENCOs in some schools are unsure of the size of their budget and if resources are not allocated to an individual child are often only able to provide intermittent or limited help.

Delegation also undermines inclusion in ACE's view. With no legal requirement to spend the funding on special educational needs, the incentive for schools to request an assessment and offer places to disabled children is removed if no extra funding accompanies a Statement.

Ofsted supports ACE's view. In its report *Inclusion: the impact of LA support and outreach services*, the inspectors say that pupils with SEN hve been denied specialist help because schools are using the money for other purposes. Lack of central funds have reduced the range and quantity of specialist help and uncertainty about funding has hampered planning, says the report. The findings were based on inspections in 2003/4 and visits to six LAs. Inspectors found that local authority support services promoted inclusion and improved the life chancs of many vulnerable pupils. They were valued by mainstream schools for providing expertise not normally available to them. However, money for schools was often not enough to allow them to buy the support pupils needed while other schools got cash, despite not having pupils needing support.

Parents still have the right to request a statutory assessment – if they know about it. But increasingly they have to appeal to the Special Educational Needs and Disability Tribunal to make local authorities carry out their legal duties. This disadvantages parents without the knowledge, stamina, confidence or support to pursue their rights. There is no right to free legal representation for Tribunal cases.

This handbook is published to ensure that as many parents as possible are in the know and that those who advise them also have a clear picture of the law. It also aims to provide a useful reference for those professionals in schools who are confused by local policies into thinking assessment and statementing is a thing of the past and for those who work in local authorities who want to support children and young people effectively. Whether you're a professional working to get the right educational support for children in the care system or a statementing officer who wants to draft good Statements and work with parents, we hope you will find this a useful reference.

Chapter one
The legal framework

While many children will have some form of learning difficulty at some stage in their lives, only a small percentage will require a statutory assessment and Statement of special educational needs (SEN).

For those children the law provides important rights and safeguards. In this chapter we describe the basic legal duties of all those concerned with the education of children with special educational needs.

If you're looking for practical information on school support, assessment or statementing, you can skip this chapter and begin with Chapters 2, 3 or 4. But remember that much of what you read later in the book is based on the legal rights and responsibilities described here.

The law

The law on special education for England and Wales is contained in **Part 1V and Schedules 26 and 27 of the Education Act 1996 (EA96)** amended by the **Special Educational Needs and Disability Act 2001 (SENDA)**. Regulations, which can be different for England and Wales, detail many of the procedures which must be carried out.

Key legal definitions in SEN

Part IV of the **Education Act 1996** opens with the key definitions relating to the law on special education. "A child has special educational needs for the purposes of this Act if he has a learning difficulty which calls for special educational provision to be made for him" (**S312 (1) EA96**).

Learning difficulties

The Act says that a child has a learning difficulty if he has:

"a) significantly greater difficulty in learning than the majority of children of his age,

b) a disability which either prevents or hinders him from making use of educational facilities of a kind generally provided for children of his age in schools within the area of the local education authority, or

c) he is under the age of five and is, or would be if special educational provision were not made for him, likely to fall within paragraph a) or b) when of or over that age". (**S312 (2) EA96**)

For children aged under two, special educational provision means any educational provision (**S312 (4)(b)**).

For children aged two and over it means "educational provision which is additional to, or otherwise different from, the educational provision made generally for children of his age in schools maintained by the local education authority (other than special schools)". (**S312 (4)(a) EA96**)

A child whose home language (or form of language) is different from that in which he will be taught is not to be taken as having a learning difficulty for that reason alone (**S312(3) EA96**).

The guidance

Statutory guidance on the law and good practice is given in the SEN Code of Practice. There is a separate code for England and Wales. In this handbook references generally apply to both codes as there are only a small number of differences between them.

For information on how to get copies, see page 127. Other guidance is also listed at the end of the book.

Local authorities (LAs) (sometimes called children's services authorities or children's trusts) and governing bodies of maintained schools and any people working with them under the Act, including health and social services, must "have regard to the provisions of the Code". The expression "have regard" means that those to whom the Code applies have a statutory duty to consider it; they must not ignore it. The government has said that if these bodies choose to do things differently they must justify any departure from the Code's advice and show that their alternative action is at least as beneficial. Failure to follow guidance without good cause may be held to be unreasonable.

Any authority or person providing funded nursery education and anyone employed by them must also have regard to the Code of Practice (**S4 The Nursery Education and Grant Maintained Schools Act 1996**). For the purpose of the Code, the term governing body is taken to include pre-school management committees and proprietors.

Academies are required as a condition of their funding to have regard to the SEN Code of Practices and to the Secretary of State's guidance on inclusion, *Inclusive Schooling: Children with Special Educational Needs*. The funding agreements drawn up by the Department for Education and Skills (DfES) also include requirements on academies which mirror the specific provisions of **S317** of the **1996 Act** which cover the duties of governing bodies to children with SEN. (*See page 18.*) Each academy must agree its policy on SEN with the Secretary of State; the policy will then be set out in an annex to the funding agreement. Since they are also tied into admission law and guidance by their funding agreement with government, academies are expected to admit pupils with SEN and disabilities as appropriate.

The SEN and Disability Tribunal must also have regard to any provision on the Code which appears to them to be relevant to any question arising on an appeal they are hearing (S313 (3) EA96).

Fundamental principles of the Code

The Code of Practice establishes some fundamental principles concerning the education of children with special needs. Summarised, these state that:
- the needs of all pupils who have SEN must be met
- most children with SEN will be educated in ordinary schools and pre-schools
- the views of the child should be sought and taken into account
- parents have a vital role to play in supporting their child's education
- children with SEN should be offered full access to a broad, balanced and relevant curriculum, including an appropriate curriculum for the foundation stage and the National Curriculum.

Principles in action

To meet these principles, local authorities and governing bodies should have procedures and practices which ensure that:

- the school culture. practice, management and uses of resources are focused on meeting all childrens needs
- a child's educational needs should be identified early
- best practice should inform the way help is planned
- views of children and parents are taken into account and professionals work in partnership with parents
- extra help should be reviewed regularly "to assess their impact, the child's progress and the views of the child, their teachers and their parents"
- local authorities should make assessments and Statements within the time limits
- local authorities should write Statements which are clear and detailed, specify monitoring arrangements and are reviewed annually
- a multi-disciplinary approach should be taken by all the agencies.

Who has responsibility for children with SEN?

Parents, local authorities, schools and early years settings all have duties with regard to the education of children with special educational needs (SEN).

Parents' duties

Parents' basic duty is set down in **Section 7** of the **Education Act 1996**:
"The parent of every child of compulsory school age shall cause him to receive efficient full-time education suitable –
a) to his age ability and aptitude, and
b) to any special educational needs he may have, either by regular attendance at school or otherwise."

Local authority duties

A local authority's most basic duty is to make sure there are sufficient schools *"in number, character and equipment to provide for all pupils the opportunity of appropriate education." "Appropriate education" should offer "such variety of instruction and training as may be desirable in view of:*
a) the pupils' different ages, abilities and aptitudes, and
b) the different periods for which they maybe expected to remain at school, including practical instruction and training appropriate to their different needs." (S14 EA96)

Local authorities responsible for making educational provision for children with special educational needs have a qualified duty to see that this takes place in mainstream schools where parents wish it as long as this is compatible with the provision of efficient education for other children (S316 EA96). (*See Chapter 4 for more on this.*)

Special educational provision can be made outside school (**S319 EA96**) and outside England and Wales (**S320 EA96**) for certain children, if this is considered appropriate.

> **Local authorities' key SEN duties are to:**
> - identify and assess children with SEN in their area whose help must be determined by the LA
> - make and maintain Statements when necessary
> - arrange the special education provision set out in a Statement
> - review the special educational provision made by the LA
> - have a SEN policy
> - provide and publicise a parent partnership service and mediation services.

LA duty to identify children with SEN

Children aged two and over

Local authorities are responsible for identifying those children in their area who will need special educational provision to be determined by the authority. This duty applies to those children for whom the local authority is 'responsible' – i.e. children (defined as anyone under 19) in their area who are:

registered at a maintained school

or

are educated at the authority's expense at a school which is not maintained

or

while not coming in the previous two categories are registered at a school and have been brought to the authority's attention as having (or probably having) special education needs.

or

are not registered at a school and are aged two or over but are not over compulsory school age and have been brought to the authority's attention as having (or probably having) special educational needs (S321 EA96).

Once identified as one of the above, children must be assessed in accordance with the detailed procedures laid down in the **1996 Act (S323 and Sched. 26)** – and after taking account of parents' views. Assessment may lead to the authority making a Statement of special educational needs. These procedures are described in full in Chapters 3 and 4.

Children under two

The position for under twos is different. Local authorities' duties to identify and provide for children aged under two apply only with parents' consent. If parents request an assessment the authority must comply, although a Statement will not necessarily be made **(S331 EA96).**

Assessments of these very young children can be carried out and Statements of SEN made and maintained in whatever way the local authority considers appropriate. The detailed duties to involve parents in the making of Statements only apply to Statements made for children aged two and over.

Co-ordinating role

The **Education Act 1996** places a duty on local authorities to keep under review their arrangements for special educational provision and to consult with the governing bodies of schools in their area (S315 EA96). This is a general co-ordinating duty and does not imply any duty to specific individual pupils.

Other authorities' duties

The local authority can request help from any health authority, primary care trust or local authority in the exercise of its duties towards children with special needs. Although they must normally comply with requests for help which they agree are necessary, health authorities and trusts can refuse to help if, in their view, the cost would be unreasonable; local authorities can refuse if a request would prevent or seriously hamper them carrying out their own duties (S322 EA96). Local authorities have no power to require these other authorities to change the spending priorities they have set in order to make provision

Local authority duty to provide information

Local authorities must make sure that advice and information is provided for parents of children with special educational needs in their area – a duty fulfilled in the main through local authority parent partnership services (**S332A**).

Local authorities have specific duties to publish information about SEN provision. These duties are set out in detail in Regulations. The information has to be provided in writing to any interested health authority or social services authority and to any person on request. The information must also be made available on local council websites. Local authorities must revise their information when significant changes occur and local schools must be told of the revisions by post or e-mail.

What must be published?

Local authorities must provide information about any plans, objectives and timescales, in particular about:

1. SEN provision which local maintained schools are expected to provide from their own funds and the provision which the authority will fund.
2. Arrangements for identifying, organising and monitoring assessment and provision for children with special educational needs, including making and maintaining Statements.
3. How they monitor the admission of children with special educational needs to local maintained schools.

(A report by the NfER for the DfES found that LEAs rarely monitored admissions of children with SEN but without Statements.) Admissions and Exclusions of Pupils with SEN, Anne Wilkin et al, NfER Research Report 608, 2005)

4. How they provide support to schools in their area in relation to special educational needs provision.
5. How they audit, plan, monitor and review provision for children with special educational needs, both generally and in relation to individual children.
6. How they secure training, advice and support for staff working in their area with children with special educational needs.

Local authorities must also describe the broad aims of their SEN policies and information about action taken to:

1. promote high standards of education for children with special educational needs
2. encourage children with SEN to participate fully in their school and community and to take part in decisions about their education
3. encourage schools in their area to share their practice in making SEN provision
4. work with other statutory and voluntary bodies to provide support for children with SEN.

The Special Educational Needs (Provision of Information by LEAs) (England) Regulations 2001 (SI 2218) see back of the SEN Code of Practice
The Special Educational Needs (Provision of Information by LEAs) (Wales) Regulations 2002 (SI 157 (W23)) see www.wales-legislation.hmso.gov.uk

(R v Brent and Harrow HA ex parte Harrow 1997 [ELR 1997 187]). This does not absolve the local authority responsible for the child from making the necessary provision, however. The courts have held that the local authority cannot delegate its legal responsibility "owed personally to the child". (R v London Borough of Harrow ex parte M 1996 [ELR 1997 62]).

Social services have general duties under a separate Act, the Children Act 1989. This Act requires local authorities to take reasonable steps to identify the extent to which there are children in need in their area. They may decide to undertake a child in need assessment at the same time as the local authority is carrying out a statutory assessment although not all children with SEN will be children in need. Social services must also publish information about the services they provide and, where they consider it appropriate, information about similar services provided by other agencies such as voluntary organisations (Para.1, Sched.2. Children Act 1989).

Social services should designate an officer or officers responsible for working with schools and local authorities on behalf of children with SEN and to whom schools and local authorities should refer for advice (COP 10.29). The officer should co-ordinate the social services advice for a statutory assessment and participate in multi-agency meetings on assessments and making Statements. The officer should ensure that schools have a contact for seeking social work advice on pupils who may have SEN.

The designated medical officer should co-ordinate the health services' advice for a statutory assessment and co-ordinate provision to be made by the health services for a child with SEN. The officer should ensure that schools have a contact – usually the school health service – for seeking medical advice on pupils. (COP 10.26)

A health authority, primary care trust or National Health Service trust have a duty to notify parents and the local authority if they are of the opinion that a child under the age of five has, or is likely to have, special educational needs. (S332 EA96)

Health authorities must normally comply with requests for help from social services in providing services for children in need (S27 Children Act 1989).

Health authorities and NHS trusts have a duty to notify parents and the local authority if they are of the opinion that a child under five has, or is likely to have, special educational needs (S332 EA96). They must give parents the names of voluntary organisations that might help when they consider that a child under five may have special educational needs (S332 (3) EA96).

The role of the Connexions service and the Learning and Skills Council are described in Chapters 5 and 8.

Governing bodies' duties

Section 317 of the Education Act 1996 (amended by the SENDA 2001) spells out the responsibilities that all governors have towards any children in their school who have special educational needs as well as general duties with regard to special education. These apply equally to governors of all maintained schools (and are mirrored in the agreements which academies make with government). The responsibilities are listed below.
The governing body must:
● do its best to ensure that the necessary provision is made for any pupil who has special educational needs;

> The 'responsible person' means the head-teacher or the appropriate governor, who may be the chair of the governors or any other another governor designated by the governing body for that purpose. In a nursery school, the responsible person is the head-teacher.

- make sure that, where the headteacher or the appropriate governor (the 'responsible person'*) has been informed by the local authority that a pupil has special educational needs, those needs are made known to all who are likely to teach him or her;
- ensure that teachers in the school are aware of the importance of identifying and providing for pupils with special educational needs;
- consult with the local authority and other bodies over special needs provision where this is desirable;
- ensure that a pupil with special educational needs joins in school activities with pupils who do not have such needs, so far as is reasonably practical and compatible with the pupil receiving the necessary special education, the efficient education of other children in the school and the efficient use of resources;
- ensure that when a child begins receiving provision for special educational needs, his or her parents are informed. This duty may be delegated to the headteacher.
S317 EA96

The school's special needs policy

The SEN information Regulations for England and Wales require all governing bodies to publish their policy on special education and to make it available free of charge to parents and prospective parents. The SEN Code of Practice says that governing bodies should, with the head, decide the school's general policy and approach to meeting pupils' special educational needs.

The policy must describe the procedures the school uses to identify, provide for and monitor provision for children with special needs.

The SEN policy must contain:

1) Basic information about the school's special educational provision:
- the objectives of the policy
- the name of the school's SEN co-ordinator (SENCO) or teacher responsible for the day-to-day operation of the SEN policy
- the arrangements for co-ordinating educational provision for pupils with SEN
- admissions arrangements
- any SEN specialism and any special units
- any facilities for pupils with SEN including those which increase or assist access.

2) Information about the school's policies for identification, assessment and provision for all pupils with SEN:
- the allocation of resources to and amongst pupils with SEN
- identification, assessment and review procedures
- arrangements for providing access to the curriculum for pupils with SEN
- how children with SEN are integrated into the school as a whole
- criteria for evaluating the success of the SEN policy
- any arrangements for considering parents' complaints about SEN provision within the school.

3) Information about the school's staffing policies and partnership with bodies beyond the school:
- the school's arrangements for SEN in-service training for staff

**ACE advice
for governors**
In your report on the way
the SEN policy has been
implemented, consider
using diagrams showing
the proportion of the
SEN budget allocated to
each stage of special
help alongside informa-
tion about actual sums
spent and total resources
available.

- use made of teachers and facilities from outside the school including support services
- arrangements for partnership with parents
- links with other mainstream and special schools, including arrangements when pupils change or leave school
- links with health and social services, educational welfare services and any voluntary organisations.

The Education (SEN) (Information) (England) Regulations 1999 (SI 2506) and The Education (SEN) (Information) (Wales) Regulations 1999 (SI 1442).

Under the **Special Educational Needs and Disability Act 2001** schools must provide the following information:
- arrangements for admission of disabled pupils
- steps taken to prevent disabled pupils from being treated less favourably than other pupils
- facilities provided to assist access to the school by disabled pupils
- details of the accessibility plan prepared by the governing body under 28D SENDA.

Information for parents in England

The **Education Act 2005** changes the way parents in England will receive information about their child's school. Instead of a governors' annual report, standardised information will appear on a national website giving details of all maintained schools in the form of a School Profile (S104 EA05). Some schools may choose to provide information about special educational needs and the school's action to support disabled pupils in their School Profile, but this gen-erally will now be found only in the school prospectus.

Under new Regulations, information previously available in the annual report is now to be included in the school prospectus. Schools are required to include a report in their prospectus on the requirements listed above, namely: i) arrangements for the admission of pupils with disabilities; ii) steps taken to prevent disabled pupils being treated less favourably thn other pupils; iii) facilities provided to assist access to the school by disabled pupils; iv) the school's accessibility plan covering future policies for increasing access of dis-abled pupils. The government has decided to deregulate the school prospectus so other information, for example, on admissions, including admission of pupils with SEN but no statement, may only be available in future via the local authority's composite prospectus of local schools. However, it appears that requirements to provide information in the prospectus about the implementa-tion of the governing body's SEN policy and any changes to that policy dur-ing the previous year will still be required.

The Education (SEN) (Information) (England) Regulations 1999 (SI 2506)); and The Education (School Information) (England) Regulations 2002 (SI 2897) amended by the Education (School Information) (England) (Amendment Regulations 2005 (SI 2152)

Information for parents in Wales

Welsh governing bodies will continue to have an annual report and hold an annual meeting with parents. Regulations require them to report on information about admissions, provide a summary of the SEN policy, details of how SEN resources have been allocated, and report on the success of their SEN policies, any significant changes to the policy and the outcome of any local consultations about SEN provision.

Sched.4 of The Education (SEN) (Information) (Wales) Regulations 1999 (SI 1442) and The School Governors' Annual Reports (Wales) Regulations 2001 (SI 1110) (W54)

As well as a summary of the SEN policy (*see above*) the school prospectus in Wales must include information about disabled pupils. This must include details of special arrangements for their admission and for enabling them to have access to any part of the school premises. Details of any steps which have been taken to prevent disabled pupils from being treated less favourably than pupils who are not disabled must also appear in the school prospectus.

Governing bodies in Wales also have a duty to promote equal opportunities. Their school prospectuses must include details of equal opportunities policies.

Education (School Information) (Wales) Regulations 1999 SI 1812

Other relevant legislation

The Children Act 1989

This legislation made radical changes in the law relating to children and to the ways in which the courts hear all kinds of cases affecting children. It covers much of the law relating to the care and upbringing of children and the social services to be provided for them. It deals with the principles which must guide the courts when making decisions relating to children in a wide range of proceedings and puts into effect provisions which are designed to ensure that the child's welfare is paramount in deciding all questions about his or her upbringing. The Act provides a definition of 'children in need' which includes disabled children.

Parents and schools were affected by the legislation particularly in connection with the new understanding of 'parental responsibility'.

The Children Act 2004

This Act restates the principle of statutory services working together to provide more coherent provision for children. In particular the Act places a duty on local authorities to make arrangements through which key agencies co-operate to improve the well-being of children and young people and widen services' powers to pool budgets in support of this.

A key principle in making those arrangements is the need to have regard to the importance of parent and carers in improving the well-being of children (S10(3)CA04).

The government aims to integrate key services for children within a single organisation – these may be called children's services authorities (CSA) or children's trusts. Most areas should have them by 2006.

The key services that should be within a CSA or trust are:

● **Local education authority** - potentially all education functions, including the education welfare service, youth service, SEN and educational psychology, childcare and early years education, and school improvement.

● **Children's social services** including assessment and services for children in need such as family support, foster and residential care, adoption services, childcare for children in need, advocacy services and child protection, and services for care leavers.

- **Community and acute health services**, such as community paediatrics, Drug Action Teams, Children's and Young People's Joint Commissioning Groups, teenage pregnancy coordinators, and locally commissioned and provided Child and Adolescent Mental Health Services. They could also include speech and language therapy, health visiting and occupational therapy services concerned with children and families. Primary care trusts will be able to delegate functions into the children's trust, and will be able to pool funds with the local authority.

Information sharing

The Act also provides the framework for the establishment of information sharing systems. This links directly to the co-operation duties on local authorities, other bodies and individual service providers and to the duties to safeguard and promote the welfare of children that are placed on agencies under this Act and on local education authorities, schools and colleges through the **Education Act 2002 (S175)**.

Where more than one agency is involved with a family, professionals are expected to share information before meeting them. Parents should be asked beforehand for permission for information about their child to be shared.

The Education Act 2005

As well as introducing the School Profile (*see page 14*), this Act makes important changes to the inspection of schools. Under the new arrangements, inspectors will be checking that schools are meeting the needs of a range of pupils, paticularly vulnerable children including those with SEN, and that they are contributing to the well-being of pupils. This relates to the five outcomes set out in the *Every Child Matters* agenda (*see page 4*). These are that children should be healthy, stay safe, enjoy and achieve, make a positive contribution to society and achieve economic well-being.

Self evaluation is at the heart of the new inspection system, so governing bodies will need to take a lead in monitoring SEN provision, identifying any weaknesses and showing that they are taking effective action. Inspectors will be looking at how the school works with parents and schools can demonstrate their commitment to partnership with parents through their SEN procedures. Local authorities will also be set targets for the achievement of pupils with SEN by the Secretary of State under regulations made under S102 of the Act.

Other assessments

As well as statutory assessment for SEN described in this book, families face a bewildering range of assessments and may misunderstand which their child and family have been through. We list here some of those additional or alternative assessments they may encounter once their child has been diagnosed as being disabled or having SEN.

Common Assessment Framework (CAF): although not in place at the time of writing, the CAF is a new assessment which increasingly will be the first contact families have with professionals. It is intended to be used by workers across health, social services and education in relation to all ages of children and young people. Unlike statutory assessment of special educational needs under the **Education Act 1996**, it does not give parents rights to initiate the process or appeal the outcome, nor does it give the child any legal entitlement to the help which has been agreed.

Children in Need Assessments: the procedures to be adopted by local authorities and health authorities when assessing the needs of children in need are not specified in the **Children Act 1989.** Professionals are guided by the *Framework for the Assessment of Children in Need and their Families* (jointly issued by the Department of Health, the Department for Education and Employment and the Home Office, 2000). Department of Health practice guidance to the Framework says that *"The assessment of a disabled child must address the needs of the parent/carers. Recognising the needs of parent/carers is a core component in agreeing services which will promote the welfare of the disabled child".*

The **Children Act 1989** empowers social services to combine assessments under the Act with those under other legislation such as the Education Act 1996, described in this handbook, the **Disabled Persons Act 1986,** and the **Chronically Sick and Disabled Persons Act 1970.**

When a young person with special educational needs moves into further education or training the Connexions service is expected to carry out a needs and provision assessment **(S140 Learning and Skills Act 2000).**

Schools are expected to carry out an initial assessment of needs to help the local authority plan appropriate provision for young people who have been permanently excluded from school. Assessment is also recommended before reintegration to school and this may be carried out "formally by an appropriate teacher or other professional," according to exclusions guidance, "or may be conducted by gathering and reviewing information held on the pupil's records and through discussion with parents".

Different types of school

Within the maintained or state-funded sector there are four main types of school: community, voluntary controlled, voluntary aided and foundation. In addition there are other categories which include special schools, nursery schools and a small number of 'independent' state schools – city technology colleges, a city college of technology of the arts and academies.

Community schools are provided by the local authority which owns the school building, employs the staff (jointly with the governors) and is responsible for admissions.

Voluntary schools can be of two types (voluntary aided and voluntary controlled). They were originally founded by voluntary organisations (usually churches).

Voluntary aided schools have a greater independence from the local authority than community and controlled schools. The governors draw up the admission criteria within government guidelines and employ the staff. Religious education and worship may be denominational.

Voluntary controlled schools are wholly financed by the local authority and are run almost exactly like community schools except there will be some representation of the voluntary body among the governors and religious education may be in accordance with their particular faith if parents ask for it.

Foundation schools are former county or voluntary schools which 'opted out' of local authority control and became grant-maintained schools. When these were abolished most became foundation schools, once again receiving their funding via the local authority, but retaining control of their own admissions and employment of staff.

Special schools are schools that cater wholly for pupils with special educational needs. They may be maintained by the local authority or be non-maintained (usually run by charities) or they could be privately run.

Nursery schools or early years settings are for children under the age of five. They may be within the maintained (i.e. state) sector or privately funded. Some private nurseries receive grants as part of local Early Years Development and Childcare Plans and provide free part-time places for three and four-year-olds.

Portage schemes provide a home visiting educational service for pre-school children who have SEN and/or a disability.

City Colleges: city technology colleges (CTCs), city college for technology of the arts (CCTA) and academies are funded jointly by the government and private sponsorship and operate as independent state schools working to rules drawn up between them and the government. Academies are set up to replace failing schools or where a new school is needed. They specialise in particular curriculum areas in the same way as schools taking part in the specialist schools programme.
Under their funding agreements with the Secretary of State, academies must have regard to the *SEN Code* and *Inclusive Schooling* guidance, DfES 2001. They are expected to admit a child when the school is named on the child's Statement but this cannot be enforced by the SEN and Disability Tribunal because of their independent status. Where a local authority proposes to name an academy in a Statement, the academy shall consent to being named, except where admitting the child would be incompatible with the provision of efficient education for other children and where no reasonable steps may be made to secure compatibility.
   The funding agreement with academies also covers information which they must provide in the prospectus about the governing body's policy for pupils with SEN i.e. information detailed in **Schedule 1** of the **Education (SEN) (Information) (Regulations) 1999** as amended.
   CTCs and CCTAs are strongly encouraged to have regard to the inclusion guidance but may operate admission criteria which all pupils, including those with SEN, must satisfy.

Specialist schools Specialist schools or colleges are generally comprehensives which can specialise in different curriculum areas. They may select up to ten per cent of their pupils on the basis of aptitude in those specialisms. Few do select, and those that do may not select the remaining 90% of their pupils.

Independent schools (sometimes called private schools) are independent of both local and central government and are not covered by much of the law governing schools. Disability discrimination law does apply, however. (*See also page 113*.)

Chapter two
The role of the school

ACE advice
for schools

Provision for pupils with special educational needs (SEN) is a matter for the school as a whole. The headteacher, SEN Co-ordinator (SENCO) and all other members of staff have important responsibilities in addition to those of the governing body described in Chapter One.

Barriers to learning may stem from school practices and policies. Check for any patterns in the school's identification and recording of children's special educational needs and parents' expressions of concern.

Identifying SEN

Many children coming into school will already have been identified as having special educational needs. Other children may have special educational needs which have gone undetected. Starting or transferring schools often provides an opportunity for SEN to be identified. Sometimes parents or young people themselves will raise their worries with teachers. Parents have a unique understanding of their child and schools are advised in the *SEN Code of Practice* (COP) to be open and responsive to this and take account of any information they provide (**COP 5.14, 6.13**). At the end of this chapter we advise parents on how to go about "expressing a concern".

At both primary and secondary level, the Code emphasises the importance of early identification (**COP 5.11, 6.10**) and suggests schools measure children's progress by:

- teacher observation and assessment
- progress against the objectives of the national literacy and numeracy strategies
- performance in the end of key stage tests and assessments of the National Curriculum
- standardised screening or assessment tools.

Children learn at different speeds and not all children learn in the same way. The National Curriculum allows for different teaching methods and for children to be taught at different levels. This is called differentiation. Children making adequate progress through differentiated teaching alone may not have learning difficulties. The legal definition of learning difficulties is given in Chapter One.

Differentiation

When a teacher differentiates, s/he may:

- Give work at a more basic and simple level
- Use teaching methods that suit a child's learning style
- Use books and worksheets that fit the child's own experiences
- Move the child into a different set or into a small group.

Is progress adequate?

Those children "whose overall attainments or attainment in specific subjects fall significantly outside the expected range may have special educational needs." (**COP 5.5, 6.5**).

The Code says that the key test for action is evidence that progress is inadequate. Adequate progress is defined as follows:

- if the gap in the child's achievement compared with other children of the same age is not getting wider
- if the child is catching up with his or her peers

- if the progress is similar to those children starting from the same level even if this is below his or her peers
- if it matches or betters the child's previous rate of progress
- if the child has access to the full curriculum
- if the child's self-help, social or personal skills are improving
- if the child's behaviour is improving.

(COP 4.14, 5.42, 6.49)

and, in addition, for pupils in secondary schools:
- if the child is likely to gain appropriate accreditation
- if they are likely to take up further education, training and/or employment.

(COP 6.49)

Informing parents

If a school concludes that a child has special educational needs they must inform the child's parents that special educational provision is being made for the child because they have SEN (S317A EA96). Parents should be fully involved when their child is receiving help. The Code says they should always be consulted and kept fully informed of the action taken to help their child, and the outcome of the action (COP 4.24, 5.47, 6.56).

Getting extra help

The SEN Code of Practice provides a model that schools can follow for those children who have special educational needs but without a Statement. This provides for help to be given at two levels: School Action and School Action Plus. In early years settings the help is called Early Years Action and Early Years Action Plus. Schools need not follow the Code to the letter but they must not ignore it and whatever model they choose, it should contain two principles:
- the help should match the nature of the child's needs
- the child's needs, the action taken and the outcomes should be regularly recorded.

(COP 5.23, 6.25)

The Code recognises that there is a continuum of special education needs; it provides a model of action based on a graduated response to those needs. The Code recommends that schools make full use of school and classroom resources, bringing in increasing specialist expertise where a child's difficulties make this necessary. It emphasises that in-school help should normally be exhausted before outside resources are called in. However, a child does not need to have moved through every level of help (*see below*) before a statutory assessment is considered. Provided there is sufficient evidence of need, a local authority can agree to undertake a statutory assessment at any stage.

Government guidance points out that *"additional help should be provided as soon as it is required rather than wait to be allocated after a period of failure". (The Distribution of Resources to Support Inclusion,2001)*

School Action

In School Action the child should be given support that is either extra to and/or different from that which the school gives through differentiated teaching.

What triggers School Action? The concern of a teacher or another person, such as the parent, backed up by evidence that a child is making little or no progress despite a differentiated curriculum, targeted teaching help, the school's usual behaviour management techniques or the use of specialist equipment. Schools are expected to investigate parents' concerns in the same way as those of teachers (COP 7.48).

In primary and secondary schools, difficulties in acquiring literacy and maths skills leading to poor attainment in some curriculum areas should also trigger School Action.

In early years settings, if the child is working at a much lower level in some areas than similar aged children, or requires specific individual help for communication and/or interaction difficulties, the setting should begin giving help at Early Years Action.

Who decides? The school consults with the parent. If the school decides that the child may need more support, the SENCO and appropriate teachers collect all available information about the child (including from the parent). Then they decide what help is needed. This should be described on an Individual Education Plan (IEP) (*see page 22*).

Provision at School Action: the Code gives as examples:
- different learning materials
- special equipment
- group or individual support such as an individualised behaviour management programme
- more adult time for planning help and monitoring its effectiveness
- training for staff to enable them to help the child better.

Although outside help is usually sought at the Action Plus level, the Code recommends speedy access for schools to local authority support services for one-off or occasional advice on strategies or equipment or for staff training (COP 5.49, 6.57, 10.13).

An outside specialist may be called in when difficulties are emerging to advise schools on effective help to prevent further problems or the development of more significant needs.

School Action Plus

Schools should always consult outside specialists when a child needs more help than is normally provided at School Action.

What triggers School Action Plus? The Code says more help might be needed if the child:
- makes little or no progress in specific areas over a long period
- is working at much lower levels of the National Curriculum or early years curriculum than his or her peers
- is having difficulty in developing literacy and maths skills
- has emotional or behavioural difficulties which "substantially and regularly interfere with the child's own learning or that of the class group"
- has sensory or physical needs which require additional support
- has ongoing communication or interaction difficulties which are causing substantial barriers to learning. **(COP 4.31, 5.56, 6.51)**

Who decides? After an IEP review meeting the school consults with the parent and decides that advice from external specialists is required. The specialists will advise on a new IEP with new targets and may assess the child and advise on

ACE advice for parents
Ask for a copy of the school's SEN policy so that you know what help you can expect for your child.

special strategies and learning materials. If they and the SENCO decide that further advice is needed from outside professionals parents must be asked for their consent (COP 5.60, 6.68). The SENCO should note in the child's record:

- what further advice is being sought
- support to be provided for the child in the meantime.

(COP 5.61, 6.69)

Provision at School Action Plus: the Code gives the following examples:

- different teaching approaches
- equipment and materials
- advice for teachers
- specialist teaching for the pupil
- changes to the management or organisation of the school.

Any extra help should, as far as is possible, be in the normal classroom setting (COP 5.59, 6.67).

Individual Education Plan (IEP)

At School Action and School Action Plus each child should have their own individual education plan (IEP). When a child moves from School Action to School Action Plus, they should have a new IEP with new ways of helping with their difficulties. The Code says that IEPs should include:

- three or four individual short-term targets that match the child's needs in communication, literacy, mathematics, and behaviour and social skills
- the teaching strategies to be used
- the help to be put in place – only help which is additional to or different from the help the school would give children not classified as having SEN
- when that help is to be reviewed
- the criteria that will be used to decide if the help has been successful or
- the criteria that will be used to decide if the help is no longer needed.

School review of IEP

The IEP should be reviewed at least twice a year and parents should be consulted. The Code says termly reviews would be best and for some pupils even more frequent reviews. The review may be at a parents' evening although government guidance in the *SEN Toolkit* suggests schools allocate extra time for parents involved in a review of an IEP. If parents are concerned about privacy, they should mention this to the school beforehand. The IEP should be discussed with the child as well as their parents. The Code recognises the child's unique knowledge and says wherever possible they should participate in the decision-making process. For very young children in particular, the Code recommends a range of techniques for consulting effectively. Use of play, art, audio and video may be appropriate as well as verbal communication.

Target
A target means the knowledge, skills and understanding which a child is expected to have by the end of a particular period
(Reg 2 SEN Regs 2001)

Early years review of IEP

IEPs for early years children should be kept continually 'under review' with regular reviews at least three times a year. These may not be formal meetings but parents' views should be sought and parents consulted throughout.

As with IEPs for children in school, they will focus on three or four key short-term targets and describe provision that is additional to or different from the pre-school's routine differentiated curriculum.

IEPS for children with Statements

The majority of pupils with Statements of SEN in mainstream or special schools are also likely to have an IEP where strategies to meet their short-term targets will complement longer-term objectives and provision in the Statement.

Outcomes

For all children with IEPs, reviews should include a record of the outcomes – successes as well as difficulties. If targets are not being met, the SEN Toolkit suggests breaking down the target even further into smaller steps or choosing an alternative target within the same area of need. It is good practice to set SMART targets, i.e. specific, measurable, achievable, relevant and time-bound (*SEN Toolkit 3.11*).

If a child is doing well, the Toolkit says that it may be possible to increase the period between reviews and consider whether the pupil's needs can be met by the school's routine differentiated curriculum. However, it reminds schools that before doing this parents should always be consulted. It also points out that for progress to be considered adequate, the targets need to be maintained so that the pupil is able to continue to perform the skill over and after a period of time.

When is an IEP not an IEP?

When it is a group education plan. The SEN Toolkit gives examples of when these might be appropriate, e.g. a local authority providing part-time group tuition for pupils with particular needs at an off-site unit, or a school withdrawing pupils for a short-term period who have similar needs and at least one target in common. However, it points out that where pupils have targets and strategies additional to the group education plan, these should be recorded in an IEP alongside details of their individual progress in both the common and individual targets.

The Toolkit points out that standardised education plans might not always be appropriate: "Pupils with similar needs will not always need the same balance of individual or group tuition, numbers of hours of in-class support or size of teaching group".

Teachers and teaching

Teachers are expected to try to give every pupil the chance *"to achieve as high a standard as possible"* (*National Curriculum Inclusion Statement*). The Inclusion Statement gives useful examples of what can be expected of teachers generally in relation to children with special educational needs. It says that teachers should teach in ways that suit pupils, for example, taking account of their learning needs and their different backgrounds and experiences. The Inclusion Statement can be found on: http://www.nc.uk.net/inclusion.html

Teachers, not the SEN co-ordinator, are responsible for making sure a child gets the help set out in their IEP. The Code says that *"all teachers are teachers of special educational needs"* and are expected to organise their lessons as part of a continuous cycle of planning, teaching, assessment and evaluation in the context of the abilities, aptitudes and interests of their pupils. Lesson planning should recognise the needs of all children as individuals.

The Code makes distinctions between its advice to primary and secondary staff; in particular, at secondary level all staff should plan and agree the arrangements for devising and recording IEPs. It points out that in some secondary schools a member of staff from each department will link up with the SENCO and co-ordinate SEN help in their departments. The Code makes these important distinctions because it is at secondary level that provision for children with SEN can unravel as many different members of staff come into contact with the child, and parents find it harder to make regular contact with the school. The Code reminds secondary schools that parents may often be the prime source of further information about their child and that they should keep them fully informed of the action taken to help their child and the outcome of the action.

Special Educational Needs Co-ordinators (SENCOs)

All mainstream schools must have a special educational needs co-ordinator (SENCO), the teacher responsible for special educational provision in the school. In small schools this may be the head. They play a key role in helping develop the SEN policy and provision in the school and take day-to-day responsibility for their operation. SENCOs' duties include:

● working closely with staff, parents and other agencies
● providing professional guidance to colleagues
● providing support and training for learning support assistants
● ensuring that records are kept on all children with SEN
● providing information for a local authority considering statutory assessment of a child
● liaising with other schools (e.g. links between secondary SENCOs and their counterparts in feeder primary schools; links between SENCOs in early years and primary schools)
● liaising with professionals from the local authority and other professionals such as Connexions personal advisers (*see page 73*)
● liaising with heads of department, pastoral colleagues and literacy and numeracy co-ordinators, curriculum co-ordinators in their own school.

Government guidance on SEN pupils in Key Stage 3, *Maximising progress: ensuring the attainment of pupils with SEN (DfES, 2005)*, says that *"SENCOs have sometimes had a peripheral role"* and that this has an impact on effective teaching and learning. It goes on to say: *"The SENCO has a key role to play as part of the school's management team to ensure that intervention maximises inclusion for pupils with SEN."*

The suggestion from the Teacher Training Agency that suitably qualified teaching assistants may undertake the SENCOs role seems at odds with this guidance. There are many excellent teaching assistants, but they have neither the qualifications or status to ensure they can exert their authority where required.

Early years

Parents of disabled children can often feel overwhelmed by the information they get when their child is newly diagnosed; or they may be concerned about getting the right provision at the right time.

The government's Early Support initiative means that in England parents in this position receive an Early Support Family Pack with information on relevant disabilities. This comes with a Family File which helps parents keep a record of key information, store relevant paperwork and list professionals who are working with them. It means families should not have to repeat their children's case history and remember everything they have been told.

Early years SENCOs

In early years settings the SENCO plans support for children with SEN in discussion with colleagues, and monitors the action taken. In the case of accredited childminders who are part of an approved network, the SENCO role maybe shared between individual childminders and the co-ordinator of the network.

Early years key worker

Under the government's Early Support initiative, children with complex needs and their families may be allocated a key worker or lead professional. If a family does not want a key worker, a professional may still be their main contact for information and guidance if they ask for it and may also offer administrative support such as inviting professionals to meetings on parents' behalf.

The key worker's main roles are to provide information to families and pass it on to other professionals as necessary and to co-ordinate the help that comes from a range of services. They should act as a contact point helping families understand 'the system' and helping them find their way through a complex network of services from benefits and transport to equipment and education.

The key worker will take responsibility for ensuring a Family Service Plan is agreed with the family and reviewed regularly. The plan is included in the Early Support Family Pack and provides a standard framework for multi-agency planning. Parents are meant to stay at "the heart of decision-making" about their child so decisions should be made in discussion with them. The Plan may list the services which will be provided and give details of who will do what but it does not bring any entitlement to services.

Although there is a much greater emphasis on joint planning between health, education and social services involving statutory, voluntary and independent providers, services will not be standardised across the country.

Early years settings

Early years settings which receive government funding must follow the law and have regard to the SEN Code of Practice. These settings will have a SENCO and are expected to have a written SEN policy.

Early years providers eligible for government funding include the full range of schools and nursery schools as well as daycare providers such as day nurseries and family centres, registered pre-schools, playgroups and private nurseries, local authority Portage schemes and accredited childminders working as part of an approved network.

Early years curriculum

In England the curriculum for early years children is called the foundation stage and the Qualifications and Curriculum Authority sets out what most children will have achieved in six areas of learning by the end of reception year (*see page 105*). The foundation stage profile is based on practitioners' ongoing observations and assessments on all six areas of learning set out in curriculum guidance for the foundation stage (www.qca.org.uk/223.html).

'Stepping stones' describe the knowledge, skills, understanding and attitudes that children need in order to achieve the early learning goals. The guidance gives 'examples of what children do', which help practitioners to identify significant developments and plan the next steps in children's learning. It also gives examples of what the practitioner needs to do to support and consolidate learning and help children make progress towards the early learning goals.

ACE advice for schools
Demonstrate your commitment to good SEN provision by including your SENCO in the senior management team.

Each child's typical developments and achievements will be recorded on assessment scales derived from the stepping stones and the early learning goals. Summary profiles must be completed for each child reaching the end of the foundation stage, four weeks before the end of the summer term.

Arrangements in Wales are similar, but the terminology is different. The six areas of learning are the same but they are called the 'Desirable Outcomes for Children's Learning before Compulsory School Age'. From five to seven children move to Key Stage 1 of the National Curriculum.

Schools in Wales may move to a foundation phase curriculum for three to seven-year-olds if a pilot being trialled in 41 early years settings between 2004 and 2008 is successful.

Help for early years children

Children are expected to progress at different rates during the foundation stage of the curriculum. For those children making slow progress, early years staff will take a graduated approach, beginning with a differentiated curriculum and progressing to further support if a child fails to make adequate progress. The help parallels that made under School Action and School Action Plus with a few differences, such as IEPs being reviewed more frequently.

Provision for early years children with SEN but no Statement is called Early Years Action and Early Years Action Plus. Parents must be told when their child begins receiving help (S123(3B) School Standards and Framework Act).

Where necessary the early years providers should bring in specialist expertise and seek advice and support from external agencies. Local authorities will check that such help has been sought when deciding whether to make a statutory assessment for a child in an early years setting. Settings may request a statutory assessment for a child aged between three and five. Parents may request a statutory assessment for their child at any age whether or not their child attends an early years setting.

The importance of parents' views being included during assessments of young children is emphasised by the Code and local authorities are encouraged to provide information to encourage their participation. This should include an explanation of what help early years settings are expected to provide and at what point the local authority would expect to make provision through a Statement. The information should include parents' rights to request a statutory assessment and appeal if refused.

Expressing a concern

If you're worried about the progress of your child you should ask for a meeting. In the first place this is likely to be with your child's class or form teacher or head of year, but if you have already told them about your concerns and are still worried, you could approach the school's SENCO or headteacher. Start by writing down in detail everything that relates to your child's special educational needs. Use the checklist at the end of Chapter 3 as a guide.

You should then write to the school asking for a meeting. You should enclose the details about your child that you have listed. The Code says schools should be open and responsive to expressions of concern from parents and take into account any information they provide. Your letter could also ask the school for the following information:

1. Does the school think my child is having any difficulty?
2. What level of the National Curriculum is my child on?
3. What do my child's test results mean?
4. Is my child at the same level as other children of the same age?
5. What sort of help is my child getting: differentiation, School Action or School Action Plus?

If you wish your child to come to the meeting and/or you would like to bring a friend or adviser along, make sure you request this in your letter.

Preparing for a meeting

It helps to be as well informed as possible when you meet the school so it may be helpful to get hold of other information:

1. The *DfES SEN Code of Practice* and *SEN Toolkit*.
   In Wales, the *SEN Code of Practice for Wales* and the *Handbook of Good Practice for Children with SEN*.
   Details on page 127 for how to get copies.
2. The school's SEN policy. Ask the headteacher or chair of governors for a copy.
3. Your child's school record which will include school reports and IEPs etc. You have a legal right to a copy within 15 school days although you may be asked to pay photocopying costs. Write to ask the governing body for this. Check through the record and make a note of anything you need to discuss or clarify at the meeting.
6. A copy of the local authority's document on what schools should give children with special educational needs. Ask your local authority's SEN Department for this or check the council website. The local authority must publish the information on their website although an ACE survey found many were not providing full information. Your local parent partnership service website may have useful information.

At the meeting

1. Take your list of worries, questions and points.
2. Tick each point as it is dealt with to ensure everything is discussed.

3. Make notes of what is said and don't be afraid to go back to a point if you feel it has not been fully sorted out.

4. Ask if you don't understand anything. Education jargon can be baffling!

5. Go back over each point at the end of the meeting to check everyone has the same understanding of what has been said or agreed.

If the school agrees that your child needs help at School Action or School Action Plus ask:

1. When will my child's IEP be drawn up? Can we meet to discuss the plan?

2. How and when will my child's progress be checked? (The school should tell you which targets it will set for your child to reach over the next few weeks) You could ask for a further meeting to discuss this. The Code says parents should be consulted as part of the IEP review process (**COP 5.53, 6.61**).

3. Will outside experts be used?

4. How can I help and be involved?

If the school disagrees that your child needs help on School Action or School Action Plus, it may be differentiating work for your child. Ask:

1. What does this mean? Setting different work? Teaching my child in a different way? Putting my child into a different group? What targets will be set?

2. Is there any further help available through differentiation or is my child getting the maximum?

3. How and when will the school check my child's progress? How and when will the school decide if progress is adequate or not and if my child has special educational needs?

4. How can I help and be involved?

After the meeting

After the meeting, write to the school with a copy of your notes to make sure everyone is clear about what has been agreed. If you realise you are unclear about any point, include your queries in the letter.

Set a date to contact the school again to check progress or review an IEP. Keep a diary about your child's progress.

If the school refuses to meet or provide you with information, you may wish to make a complaint If the school disagrees that your child needs differentiated work or has special educational needs, or says there isn't enough help to go round, you may wish to approach a more senior member of staff. Set yourself a personal deadline – say half a term – to go back to the school. If your child is still having difficulties, contact one of the organisations listed under Useful Organisations (*see pages 129 to 133*) or make a complaint (*see page 77*).

Chapter three
Statutory assessment

For some children the help that a school can normally provide will not be enough. They may require greater investigation of their difficulties to decide whether they need more or different help. This may mean a statutory assessment of their needs. **The Education (SEN) (England) (Consolidation) Regulations 2001 [SI 3455]** and **Education (SEN) (Wales) Regulations 2002 [SI 152]** set out in detail how the statutory assessment is carried out.

Local authorities must identify children who have special educational needs (SEN) and for whom it is necessary for the local authority to determine the special educational provision their learning difficulty calls for (S321 EA96). They should obtain information from maintained schools about registered pupils who live in their area and are receiving provision under School Action Plus.

Proposal to assess

The decision to assess is made by the local authority responsible for the child. Local authorities can arrive at this decision by three routes:

- after receiving a formal request from a parent (S329 (1) EA96)
- after receiving a formal request from the headteacher or proprietor of the child's school, nursery school, pupil referral unit or from relevant nursery education providers* (S329A EA96)
- after a referral. This could be from an agency such as social services or the health authority or National Health Service trust (S332 EA96).

(*Relevant early years education is nursery education provided by a local authority or other provider operating within an early years development plan. Under S123 School Standards and Framework Act, such early years settings in common with schools must have regard to the SEN Code of Practice (COP). Where we use the term early education setting or provider this refers to those nurseries receiving state funding to provide early education for three, four and five-year-olds.)

Request from parents

Parents can request an assessment (S329 EA96) or, if the child already has a Statement, they can ask for a reassessment (S328 EA96). In the case of children under two, the local authority must comply with the parents' request. Assessments of children under two need not follow the same statutory procedures which apply to assessments of older children.

For children of two and over, the local authority must comply with a parental request unless an assessment has been made within the previous six months, or unless the local authority considers an assessment is not necessary.

It is helpful if parents are clear about why they want the assessment and supply any information about any help the child has already received and any information which they have from professionals and the school who may have already been involved with helping the child. There is no requirement for par-

---

Statutory assessment

In this book we use the term statutory assessment when we are describing an assessment under the **Education Act 1996**. Sometimes people call it a 'formal assessment'. Statutory assessment is distinct from other assessments (see pages 16-17). A statutory assessment is the way the local authority decides:
- whether your child has special educational needs which may require a Statement
- what those special educational needs are
- how those special educational needs will be met.

Dear Education Officer,

I am writing to ask you to assess the educational needs of my daughter Anna under Section 323 of the 1996 Education Act.
I make this request under Section 328 of the Act (if the child already has a Statement) or 329 of the Act (if the child has no Statement) for the following reasons...
(State your reasons if you wish)

Yours faithfully
Parent

ents to provide reasons or evidence but it will help the local authority to make the right decision about whether an assessment is necessary. Parents can follow the Checklist on pages 43 and 44 and send in a report at this stage. If the local authority decides to go ahead with the assessment it will take this into account and parents will be able to add to it.

Following a request from a parent, the local authority will immediately contact them to investigate the nature of their concern and find out their views of the provision made for their child at school, where relevant. The local authority must also inform the head of the child's school of the parents' request. It will need to ask for information about the child's progress and the school's view of the child's learning difficulties.

Request from a school or early years setting

Schools can ask the local authority to make a statutory assessment but they should first consult the child's parents. The Code recommends that parents be fully involved in the discussion leading up to a school's decision to request a statutory assessment. If a school makes a request, the local authority must formally notify the parents of that fact and of their right to appeal to the Tribunal if the local authority refuses to assess. There is no appeal against a decision to *make* a statutory assessment but parents can put their views to the local authority. Whether the parent or school make the request, the local authority will alert social services and the health authority to the possibility that they may need to provide reports if the assessment goes ahead.

The local authority has six weeks to consider whether to carry out a statutory assessment and, if it decides to go ahead, it must serve a notice informing the headteacher of the help the authority is likely to request (SEN Reg 6(6)).

Definitions

In this context 'schools' mean:
● maintained schools (mainstream and special, other than special schools established in a hospital)
● maintained nursery schools
● pupil referral units
● all independent schools including academies, city technology colleges and city colleges for technology of the arts
● special schools approved by the Secretary of State under S342 of the Education Act 1996 (i.e. special schools not maintained by local authorities)
● early education settings in receipt of local authority funding who are providers of free nursery education to three, four and five-year-olds.

What triggers a request?

When a school requests a statutory assessment the pupil will have demonstrated "significant cause for concern" (COP 5.62, 6.71).

Evidence for the local authority

For most children the school should provide the local authority with a record of their help for the child including the resources or special arrangements they have already made available (COP 5.24, 6.26).

Written evidence or information should cover:
● any action taken through School Action and School Action Plus

- IEPs for the child
- records of regular reviews and their outcomes
- the child's health including their medical history where relevant
- National Curriculum levels
- attainments in literacy and mathematics
- educational and other assessments, for example from an advisory specialist support teacher or an educational psychologist
- views of the parent and the pupil
- involvement of other professionals
- any involvement by the social services or education welfare service

Cases requiring urgent action

A few children may move straight to statutory assessment where a school is aware that immediate specialist intervention is required or where a quick response is required. **(COP 7.30).** The Code gives the examples of a diagnosis of severe sensory or other impairment or where a child's severe emotional and behavioural difficulties require an urgent outside-school response. A single report from a lead professional may be sufficient where a child through ill health or an accident suddenly acquires easily identifiable complex needs that require an assessment and provision from the local authority **(COP 7.14).**

An emergency placement may be made for children requiring urgent assessment and help e.g. where
- a child's medical circumstances have changed suddenly causing a rapid and serious deterioration in the child's health or development
- the parents, school, relevant professionals and the local authority agree that a sudden and serious deterioration in the child's behaviour make the child's current placement untenable or unsafe
- where a child arriving unexpectedly in the local authority exhibits such significant learning difficulties as would normally warrant a Statement
- where a young person returns home from a secure unit or young offender institution.

(COP 8.23)

Emergency placements may be in a special school but only when the local authority, parents, school and relevant professionals agree it **(COP 8.24).** Parents should be told clearly by the local authority the reasons for the placement and its duration. Long-term decisions about the child's placement should not be prejudiced by the type of emergency placement made **(COP 8.26).** (*See also page 42.*)

Request from an early years setting

Early years settings requesting statutory assessment for a child aged between three and five should provide the local authority with information:
- about the child's difficulties identified by the early years workers
- about the strategies used through Early Years Action and/or Early Years Action Plus
- about any outside advice which has been sought regarding the child's physical health, communication skills, perceptual and motor skills, self-help skills, social skills and emotional and behavioural development.

The local authority will seek similar information to that listed for schools (*above*) including the views of parents and any copies of IEPs produced by the

ACE advice to parents
ACE advises parents to send their own letter asking for a statutory assessment to the local authority even if the school has decided to do so. It makes no difference to your legal rights – the time limits and appeal rights apply whether you or the school makes the request. However, it does mean you can be sure of the exact date that the request goes in and that a statutory assessment, not just an informal assessment, has been requested. Use the model letter on page 30.

early years setting. For some very young children with severe and complex needs the local authority may rely on a single report from the lead professional involved with the child (COP 7.14).

Referral by another agency

Health and social services may draw children to the local authority's attention but have no statutory right to request an assessment. Under fives with complex needs who are not yet attending school are most likely to be referred to their local authority in this way. The legal six weeks time period by which the local authority must inform parents and schools of a decision to assess or not does not apply to cases which have been referred in this way. Nor do parents have the right of appeal if the local authority refuses to assess after such a referral. This means it would be advisable for parents to make a formal request themselves to ensure their full rights. (See model letter page 30.)

Formal notice from the local authority

In cases where someone other than a parent has requested statutory assessment of a child, the local authority must notify the parents. The authority:

- must write to the parents to give them notice that they are consider ing making a statutory assessment. At this stage the local authority must make it clear that it has not made a decision either way.
- must set out for parents the procedures for statutory assessment and drawing up of a Statement if they go ahead.
- should explain the legal time limits at each stage of the procedure and explain how parents can help the local authority meet the time limits. They should explain the exceptions to the time limits.
- must tell parents the name of the local authority officer who can provide further information. This person may be known as the Named Officer.
- must tell parents of their right to write or explain in person to say why they believe their child should or should not be assessed. The local authority must set a time limit of no less than 29 days for receipt of parents' views.
- should encourage parents to contribute and, where parents discuss their views with the local authority, agree a written summary of those views with them. To avoid delays, the local authority could ask parents to formally let them know if they do not wish to say or write anything.
- must give parents information about the local parent partnership service which should tell parents about sources of independent advice, such as local or national voluntary organisations and support groups.
- should ask parents if they would like the local authority to consult anyone about their child in addition to those whom the local authority must approach for educational, medical, psychological and social services advice if the local authority decides to go ahead with the statutory assessment.
- should tell parents that any private advice or opinions they provide will be taken into account.

The local authority must also send a copy of the notice to the social services and the health authority explaining that they will be asked for advice if they decide to carry out the assessment. It should also supply a copy to its own educational psychology service and any other agencies who might be asked for advice if the assessment goes ahead. If the request for a statutory assessment comes from the parent, the local authority is not required to issue a formal notice to parents but it should provide the information set out above.

Parent partnership services

These are advice and information services which must be arranged by the local authority for parents of children with special educational needs – not only those with Statements. Those who run the service are usually known as parent partnership officers (PPOs). Sometimes the services will be run by the voluntary sector on the local authority's behalf but local authorities are responsible for publicising the service, funding it adequately and ensuring it is properly run.

Although independent of the decision-making process, PPOs may take a neutral stance while others may be prepared to take on advocacy for childen and parents. Parents need to clarify this from the beginning. Local authorities and schools should always get a parent's permission before referring them to the parent partnership service or other support organisation.

The parent partnership service is expected to use its "best endeavours" to recruit and arrange training of sufficient Independent Parental Supporters (IPS) to meet the needs of parents in their area. The IPS is usually an unpaid volunteer who should support parents by attending meetings, encouraging parental participation and helping to explain the SEN framework.

Time limits

If a parent or school requests a statutory assessment, the local authority must decide within six weeks of receiving the request whether to carry out such an assessment.

If the local authority notifies parents that it intends making an assessment, it must decide within six weeks of the notification.

Parents have 29 days to **make representations** and that is part of the six weeks.

Carrying out the **statutory assessment** should take no longer than ten weeks. The period begins when the local authority makes its decision to assess and ends when it decides whether or not to make a Statement.

If the local authority decides to issue a Statement it must draft a **proposed Statement** within two weeks.

Unless parents request more than one meeting, the **final Statement** must be issued within eight weeks of them receiving the proposed Statement. If there are no delays, the whole process should take no more than 26 weeks.

Deciding whether to assess

Although the Code says that each case should be looked at individually, it gives general guidelines for local authorities on when to consider statutory assessment. For a school-age child the local authority will look at:

- the school's assessment of the child's difficulties and those of other professionals such as educational psychologists
- the school's action so far

Parents' checklist

Has the local authority:

clearly explained the procedures?

given you precise timings for each stage?

asked you whether or not you would like your child to be assessed?

given you the name of a local authority officer (Named Officer) who can keep you up to date with what's happening?

given you contact details for the parent partnership service?

asked you if you would like the local authority to contact anyone else about your child? (You can provide information from others who know your child but whom the local authority may not routinely consult.)

- the child's academic attainment
- the child's progress
- parental evidence.

Professionals' reports

The local authority will consider any school records which document the child's learning difficulties. These will include reports from educational psychologists and special support teachers, SENCOs and any reports from other professionals such as those working in child health or social services.

School action so far

The local authority should consider whether the school has:
- drawn up, monitored and evaluated IEPs in consultation with outside specialists
- sought the views of, and involved, the child's parents
- actively sought the views of the child
- used appropriate programmes, teaching strategies and equipment
- used pastoral care and guidance and sought external advice to help with social, emotional or behavioural difficulties
- with the parents' consent, notified and sought the help of the school doctor and/or the child's GP.

Schools may also have made some of the provision suggested in the Code for children with particular learning difficulties. The Code categorises these difficulties into four areas of need:
- communication and interaction
- cognition and learning
- behaviour, emotional and social development
- sensory and/or physical needs.
(COP 7:52)

Who provides – school or local authority?

Depending on the local funding, the provision recommended for children whose difficulties fall into the four areas of need may be made from school budgets or a local authority central funds for children with Statements. The decision about whether schools make this provision under School Action Plus or the local authority through assessment and statementing is left to local authorities.

This lack of clarity about who pays can cause difficulties for parents. The school may say it is doing all it can for their child and has no resources to do more while the local authority may say the child's difficulties are not sufficiently complex or significant to warrant statutory assessment and a Statement.

The Code recognises that children may have needs which span more than one of the four areas of need; these children's needs are described as complex and in these cases the Code says it is important that "a detailed assessment" of the pupil and their situation is carried out (COP 7:53). However, when deciding whether to carry out a *statutory* assessment local authorities will have to decide whether the child's individual needs may be met from the resources already available in schools. So, as well as complexity, the severity of the child's needs will also be a factor to be taken into consideration (COP 7:53).

Parents deciding whether to request a statutory assessment or appeal against a refusal to assess could begin by checking whether the school has done all of the things listed above (*see above:* **School action so far**). They should get hold of a copy of the local authority's SEN policy which should include the arrangements for identifying and assessing children with special educational needs. They should also request information which local authorities must publish about what special educational provision they expect local state schools to make from their own budget shares and what they expect the authority will normally pay for from its central funds. This varies from area to area although the trend is for local authorities to delegate more and more SEN funding for schools. Up-to-date information about the policy and what local schools provide must be posted on the authority's website.

(The Special Educational Needs (Provision of Information by Local Education Authorities) (England) Regulations 2001 [SI 2218]); (The Special Educational Needs (Provision of Information by Local Education Authorities) (Wales) Regulations 2002 [SI 157 W23])

Getting hold of the information may require determination. Parents tell ACE that local authorities are sometimes unsure what or where their SEN policy is, while surveys carried out by ACE of local authority websites in 2003 and 2004 found that many failed to comply with the legal requirements in the information they provided.

Parents may still be unsure if the local authority policy and information is realistic. They may need to ask the school for a copy of its SEN policy and ask for information about how resources are allocated among pupils with SEN. The school prospectus should have details. If the information is not conclusive, they may need to ask more specific questions which could be sent to the SEN governor – the governor with responsibility for SEN issues. If parents conclude that the school should be providing more help at School Action Plus, they may need to take this up with the school. The Code suggests that parent partnership services may be involved where parents have disputes with schools about special educational provision. The service may be able to intervene on their behalf or direct them to disagreement resolution services.

If parents believe the local authority should be providing the additional help they should ask for a statutory assessment (*see pages 29 and 30*). Although local authority policies are a useful way for authorities to make consistent decisions, they must look at each case on its merits. Their policies cannot over-rule their legal duty to carry out a statutory assessment where it is necessary for them to determine the extra educational help a child needs.

Child's progress and attainment

Much information about the achievement of an individual child will come from the school. This may include:
- teachers' own recorded assessments of a child's work in school
- the outcome of Individual Education Plans
- any portfolio of the child's work
- end of key stage test and assessment results
- the child's achievement in the six areas of learning for early years children (*see page 105*).

The local authority will look to see if there are
  - significant discrepancies between the child's performance and that of the

majority of children of his or her age. Is the child working at a much lower level than his peers in the core subjects of the National Curriculum or (for younger children) the foundation stage curriculum? Is the child not benefiting from the National Curriculum programmes of study and/or is falling progressively behind?

- significant discrepancies between the child's performance and that expected of the child by professionals and parents. Where possible their views should be supported by the results of standardised tests.

- significant discrepancies of the child's performance within one of the core subjects of the National Curriculum or between one of the core subjects and another. Again is the child falling behind? Can this be established by teacher assessment, standardised tests and evidence of the child's work?

- significant discrepancies between the child's attainments in early learning goals in comparison with the attainments of the majority of their peers.

(COP 7:40)

Where the balance of evidence presented to and assessed by the local authority suggests that the child's learning difficulties:

● have not responded to relevant and purposeful measures taken by the school or setting and external specialists

and

● may call for special educational provision which cannot reasonably be provided within the resources normally available to mainstream schools and settings in the area

the Code says the local authority should consider very carefully the case for a statutory assessment of the child's special educational needs.

(COP 7:50)

Other difficulties

In addition to parents' and children's views, the local authority may ask parents whether family circumstances or medical problems could be contributing to their child's difficulties. In some cases this may lead the local authority to direct the parent to other services such as health or social services, or the school attendance services (COP 7:44–7:45).The Code of Practice distinguishes between under-attainment and special educational needs but it is important to remember the legal definition of "learning difficulty" described in Chapter 1 (see page 7). "Under-attainment" is not a concept which is defined legally.

Medical needs

Children with medical needs may have special educational needs although the Code says a medical diagnosis or disability does not necessarily imply SEN. The Code acknowledges that medical conditions may have a significant impact on a child's experiences and progress in school and may directly affect their cognitive or physical abilities, their behaviour or emotional state. The impact may also be indirect, perhaps disrupting their access to education. However it, says that it will be the child's educational needs rather than a medical diagnosis that must be considered (COP 7:64–7:67).

Access to Education, statutory guidance on the education of children and young people with medical needs, says that a medical condition may increase the likelihood that a pupil has a learning difficulty as defined in law and that they may require a statutory assessment. (See also page 118.)

Other government guidance, *Managing Medicines in Schools and Early Years Settings*, recommends that a pupil with medical needs should have an individual health care plan to identify the level of support needed at school. There should be a written agreement with parents, jointly reviewed at least once a year. If a health care plan and help at School Action Plus are not enough, parents should consider asking for a statutory assessment of their child.

If parents disagree with the proposal to assess

If parents do not agree that a statutory assessment is needed or will help their child, or if they are uncertain, they should prepare their reasons and get them to the authority within the time limit of at least 29 days.

Moderation

Local authorities often use moderating groups – a multi-professional panel usually including headteachers, educational psychologists, SENCOs and other professionals – to help them make consistent decisions on which children require a statutory assessment. The Code says that at their best panels can ensure consistent and transparent decision-making but points out that their role must be "clear, public and open to scrutiny". While the panel meetings which discuss individual children will not be open to the public, parents should be told who sits on the panel, the criteria by which they make their decisions and the reasons for any decisions about their child.

The decision

Local authorities must write to the parents as quickly as possible with their decision, their reasons for it and explain how to access the parent partnership service (*see page 33*). Where the parent or school has requested the assessment and the local authority decides that an assessment is not necessary, it must also inform parents of the right of appeal to the SEN and Disability Tribunal and the time limits for such an appeal. It must also tell them of mediation services and that disagreement resolution does not affect their right to appeal (*see* **Chapter 6: Appeals and Complaints**). If the decision was made after a referral from another agency then there is no right of appeal. Parents will have to make a formal request themselves to trigger their appeal rights.

The Code recommends that following a refusal to assess, the local authority should arrange a meeting with parents and possibly the headteacher or SENCO of the child's school. This will be particularly useful where there are disagreements between parents and the school about the help needed (**COP 7.70**).

There is no statutory right of appeal against a local authority's decision to go ahead with a statutory assessment. Parents can only appeal at this stage if the local authority decides not to assess their child. However, if they feel that there are good reasons for believing that the local authority's decision is unreasonable, because it has not taken their views properly into account, or for any other reason, they can make a formal complaint to the Secretary of State for Education and Skills. The Secretary of State is only likely to intervene in exceptional circumstances, however. (*See page 91*.)

The assessment

The law sets out in great detail how assessments are to be carried out for children aged two and over, including what advice the local authority must seek about the child's special educational needs and parents' rights to be involved in the assessment.

The Code of Practice provides guidance on points of law contained in the **Education (SEN) (England) (Consolidation) Regulations 2001 [SI 3455]** or the **Education (SEN) (Wales) Regulations 2002 [SI 152 W20]** which govern the management of every stage of the assessment procedures.

The local authority must take into account any representations made by parents and any evidence submitted by, or at the request of, parents. This includes anything submitted earlier when the local authority was considering-whether to assess (**SEN Reg 7**).

The local authority must, as a minimum, seek advice from the child's parents, advice from educational, medical, psychological and social services, and "any other advice which the authority think appropriate for the purpose of arriving at a satisfactory assessment". (The local authority does not need to seek this advice if it has already been obtained in the preceding 12 months and the local authority, the person, giving the advice or the child's parent are satisfied that "the existing advice is sufficient...") (**SEN Reg 7**).

Once it decides to assess, the local authority should seek the advice immediately and ask those it has contacted to reply within six weeks. There is a ten week statutory time limit within which the local authority must complete the assessment, beginning from the date of the notice to assess. This can only be extended in exceptional circumstances (*see* **Exceptions to time limits** *page 41*).

The advice

The local authority will send copies of parents' representations and any evidence they provide to the professionals it is seeking advice from. The professional advice must set out how educational, medical, psychological or other factors affect the child's current and future educational needs and the provision that is considered appropriate in the light of those factors. Local authorities must not have blanket policies preventing professionals from commenting on the amount of provision they consider a child requires. Professionals' advice should not be influenced by consideration of the school which the child might eventually attend. Although parents and professionals may discuss the type of school which might be most appropriate, the specific school is decided later after the Statement is drafted and parents have been given an opportunity to state a preference for a school. Such discussions should not commit the local authority, nor pre-empt the parents' preference or representations (**COP 7:80**).

Parents' advice

Parents should now draw their arguments together to send in to the local authority before the deadline is up. If their child is at school and there has been full discussion and consultation with staff, they should have a great deal of information to hand. Obviously representations made by parents carry more weight with the authority if there are teachers or others involved in the child's education who agree with their views and are prepared to write in support. The child's own doctor, health visitor or social worker may be able to help. If so, parents should get them to put their views in writing and forward them to the local authority with their own report.

If parents want help with making their views known they can ask the Named Officer, the LA officer who is dealing with their child's assessment, or an Independent Parental Supporter to provide it. The officer can provide information, but for independent advice parents may want to ask the IPS or a voluntary organisation. (*See* **Parents' Checklist** *page 40.*)

Pupils' views

The local authority should also seek the child's views, remembering that children and young people may feel anxious and confused about the purpose of an assessment and need clear information about its purpose.

Parents can help by talking over what will happen with their child. Many children will be able to write down what they think about their special educational needs and how they would like them to be met. Some local authorities provide children with their own report form. Other children will be able to communicate their views in whatever way they normally communicate, and someone will be able to write down what the child communicates.

Children's views may be mediated by:
  - a parent or carer
  - a familiar professional, for example: a teacher, a social worker, a mentor
  - a support teacher for children with English as an additional language
  - an advocate.

For very young children or severely disabled children, there is a range of information that may be gleaned from careful observation of a child. Such information can supplement and complement the views that the child has expressed directly. These might be observations of:
  ● simple reflex responses
  ● different reactions to different circumstances
  ● gaze which can be interpreted by those who know the child well
  ● response to familiar people, events, objects, for example: showing pleasure when a puppet character acts in a certain way
  ● gestures, actions, for example: selecting symbols to express feelings
  ● play
  ● child's behaviour, for example: shyness, tantrums, happiness – variations at home and school
  ● child's choices, for example: friendships, activities.

There is a range of ways in which children's views may be recorded and used to inform their statutory assessment. The following are a few examples:
  ● a child's own written report of their views
  ● an audio tape recording of their views
  ● a child may communicate their views to someone else who writes them down for them
  ● a child's drawings
  ● a relevant piece of writing
  ● photos and video recordings
  ● a diary of child's responses
  ● a report of observations of a child.

Professionals' advice

To make a statutory assessment the local authority must seek the following:

Educational advice - this must be sought from the child's headteacher. If the head himself has not taught the child within the preceding 18 months, then they should consult with a teacher who has taught the child more recently. The head's advice will include the steps taken by the school to identify and assess the special educational needs of the child and to make provision to meet those needs. If the child has sensory difficulties the local authority must obtain educational advice from a teacher qualified to teach children who are visually or hearing impaired.

Educational advice would normally be from a qualified teacher but in the case of children in early years settings that may not always be possible. In those cases the person responsible for the child's education provision must be asked for advice (**SEN Reg 8**).

Medical advice must be sought from the health authority which must obtain the advice from a fully registered medical practitioner (**SEN Reg 9**).

Psychological advice - must be sought from a person regularly employed by the local authority as an educational psychologist or engaged as such for the particular case. If they are aware that another psychologist has relevant knowledge of, or information relating to a child, their advice must be given after consultation with that other psychologist (**SEN Reg 10**).

Social services advice – social services should be asked if they have information which could help in assessing the needs of a particular child. This is likely to be relevant where a child is regarded as being 'in need' as defined by the **Children Act 1989** or where a child is in public care. In the case of the latter, the school's designated teacher for 'looked after' children, as well as the child's social worker, may contribute to the assessment. The Code also advises that where a child is currently the subject of public law proceedings it would be advisable for the local authority to involve the Children's Guardian

Parents' checklist on independent reports

Sometimes a parent who is convinced that their child needs a Statement believes that the local authority is likely to decide that a statutory assessment is not necessary. If this is the situation you face it may be useful to consider if there are any professionals who will back up your case.

Are there any professionals who already know your child?

These would include doctors, consultants, teachers at previous schools, playgroup workers, health visitors. Such people could probably put together a report on your child fairly quickly and probably would not charge or would charge comparatively little.

Are there any professionals who could assess the child?

Your GP may agree to refer your child to a specialist in the health service. With younger children in particular it may have been the child health services which first told you there was a problem or which referred your child to the local authority.

The specialist **disability organisations** often know of specialists who are sympathetic to parents in this situation and who will carry out private assessments or examinations and write reports. A second opinion may be available through **IPSEA**. (See page 130.)

Professional organisations sometimes give names of their members who will do private assessments. Parents will generally be charged for these reports. If possible try to ask someone who specialises in the difficulties experienced by your child. Their views will have more weight.

An expert report may be required by a solicitor providing help to a family on low income under the **Legal Help scheme** (formerly known as Green Form advice). This allows for a limited amount of free initial legal advice from a solicitor. It can be on almost any point of English law and the help can include giving advice, writing letters, negotiating, and obtaining a barrister's opinion. You can find a solicitor with an education franchise on the Community Legal Services website: www.justask.org.uk – or contact the Education Law Association. (See page 131.)

The problem for parents is that private assessments can be very expensive and sometimes there is a long wait for an appointment. Obviously local authorities are generally more willing to accept the views of their own advisers but they must consider your representations and any evidence you want to give, including a private report (**SEN Reg 11**).

Copies of the parents' own representations and advice from any other source that they submit must be provided by the local authority to the other professionals whose advice they seek (**SEN Reg 4**).

(formerly known as the guardian ad litem) in the assessment.

Other advice – this could be advice from the Children's Education Advisory Service where the child's parent is a serving member of the armed forces, or from Sure Start professionals where a young child is involved in a programme.

Exceptions to the time limits

Local authorities must comply with the legal 10 week time limit for carrying out an assessment unless it is impractical **(SEN Reg 12 (6))**. The SEN Regulations describe the circumstances when exceptions are allowed. They are
- if, exceptionally, further advice is necessary
- if the local authority requests advice from the headteacher/SENCO during a period beginning one week before a school is closed for a continuous period of not less than four weeks from that date and ending one week before the date on which it re-opens
- if exceptional personal circumstances affect the child or his parent during the six week period when the local authority is considering making an assessment or during the ten week period when it is carrying out the assessment
- the child or his parent are absent from the area of the authority for a continuous period of not less than four weeks in either of the periods described above
- the child fails to keep an appointment for an examination or a test during the ten week assessment period
- the health authority or social services have not complied with the local authority's request within six weeks.

SEN Reg 12(7)

Health and social services must normally respond within six weeks of receiving the request for advice from the local authority. Again there are similar exceptions. Also if the health authority had no previous relevant knowledge of the child they are not obliged to keep to the six week time limit. If social services had no previous knowledge of the child they need not comply with the request at all.

SEN Reg 12(9)(10)(11)

Examinations

If a local authority decides to examine a child as part of the assessment, it must send a notice to the parents and inform them of their right to attend. The notice must state the purpose of the examination; its time and place; name a local authority official who can provide further information; explain to parents that they can submit information to the authority and that they have a right to be present **(Sched.26(4) EA96)**.

If parents do not present their child for examination at the time suggested and have no reasonable excuse, they can be taken to court and fined. (This does not apply to examinations of young people over compulsory school age.) **Sched.26(5) EA96**

The Code suggests that parents should be told that there may be certain circumstances when their presence at an examination would be counterproductive, for example, during classroom observation when a child might behave differently if their parent was present.

(*The 'responsible person' means the headteacher or the appropriate governor, who may be the chair of the governors or any other another governor designated by the governing body for that purpose. In a nursery school, the responsible person is the headteacher.)

Emergency assessment places

The majority of pupils are assessed at their mainstream school but in a very small number of exceptional cases a child may be placed in a special school during the assessment. The Code says this is where immediate or emergency support is required or where any delay might further damage the child's development. The law now allows a child to be educated in a special school without a Statement in the following exceptional circumstances:

- where the child is being assessed to determine if a Statement is needed
- where there has been a change in circumstances
- where the child is in hospital and attends a hospital special school.

S316A (2) EA96

When an emergency placement is made, the local authority should immediately initiate a statutory assessment or reassessment. If, following the assessment, the local authority decides against making a Statement the child's emergency placement should be reconsidered. If the child has been placed in a special school for an assessment and the local authority decides not to make a Statement, the child can only remain in the school for a further ten school days after parents have been notified of the decision (COP 8.25–8.26).

Reassessment

Parents of a child with a Statement may request a new assessment of a child (S328 EA96) and schools may also request a new assessment (S329A EA96). The local authority must comply unless an assessment has been made within the previous six months or the local authority concludes that it is unnecessary. In the case of the latter, if the local authority refuses, it must inform parents of its decision and that the parent may appeal. Either way, the procedures are the same as when there is a request for an assessment for a child with no Statement.

The local authority's decision

Having received all the advice, the local authority must decide whether it needs to make a Statement or amend an existing Statement. It must make that decision within ten weeks of serving the notice of statutory assessment. If it decides to go ahead, it has two weeks to provide the parents with a proposed Statement.

The local authority says no

If the local authority decides that a Statement or an amended Statement is not necessary, it must, within two weeks of finishing the assessment, notify the parents and give reasons, and should also notify the school of that decision, giving the reasons. Parents must be informed of their right of appeal, the time limits for lodging an appeal, the availability of parent partnership and disagreement resolution services and that disagreement resolution will not affect their right of appeal. Where the local authority has carried out a reassessment of a child with a Statement it must provide parents with copies of the professional advice obtained (SEN Reg 17 (2c)).

Governors and teachers at the school may be as disappointed as the parents by a local authority's decision not to make or to amend a Statement. They may argue that they cannot make any more provision than they were making before the assessment. In this situation parents can either use the authority's disagreement resolution service and/or appeal to the Tribunal against the local authority's decision. (*See Chapter 6.*)

Parents could also ask the local authority for further advice, including a Note in Lieu (*see below*), to help the school meet their child's needs. Any future programme of action to meet the child's needs should operate within the framework of the school's SEN policy. All maintained schools have clear responsibilities towards all children with special needs, including those without a Statement, and receive funding in their budgets for this.

Notes in lieu

The Code says that if the local authority decides against issuing a Statement, it is preferable that it provides a Note in Lieu within two weeks of concluding the assessment. A Note in Lieu is a document that may be issued to the child's parents and school describing the child's special educational needs, explaining why the local authority does not think it necessary to make a Statement and making recommendations about appropriate provision for the child. All the advice received during the assessment should be attached to the note sent to the parents and, with their consent, should also be sent to the child's school (COP 8.17).

The Code also recommends that local authorities arrange a meeting for parents with the Named Officer and the headteacher or SENCO of their child's school to discuss the provision to be made.

A Note in Lieu could contain as much detailed consideration and information as a Statement – and so provide parents and the school with helpful guidance in supporting the child. Even though it may follow the same format as a Statement, parents should realise, however, that the Note in Lieu has no legal status and is not binding on the school.

The statutory assessment ends when the local authority decides whether or not it will make a Statement. The next chapter examines what happens when the local authority draws up a Statement.

Parents' action: writing your advice

Advice for the assessment

It will help your child to give as much information as possible when you are asked to provide advice as part of the assessment. The following lists some of the points you should consider including.

Your child's early years

Say when you first noticed any problems – big or small. Did you tell anyone? What help or advice did you get?

Your child now

Health – eating, sleeping, illnesses, tiredness, depression, panic attacks
Physical skills – walking, climbing, drawing, using scissors
Communication – speech, describing things, talking to people, using the telephone, taking messages

Personal skills – dressing washing, dealing with pocket money, time-keeping, remembering sports kit/books etc for school
Behaviour – poor concentration, anxiety, aggression, following instructions.

Your child at home

Watching TV, reading, hobbies
Outside activities – clubs, sports
Relationships – parents, brothers and sisters, other adults
Behaviour at home – sharing, listening, helping, moods, caring, tantrums
Homework – difficulty with remembering what to do or getting it finished in the set time.

Your child at school

What is your child good at? What does your child enjoy?
Friendships, relationships with teachers
Problem areas: lessons, playtime, changing class, school transfer
Help which has worked or not worked for your child
Are your child's difficulties getting worse?
What help do you think your child needs?

Your child's view

What does your child say about their difficulties? When do they most enjoy learning?
Your child's views are important. They can give first-hand reports of the difficulties they have and how the help they get at school works for them. Their behaviour usually shows what they feel about something.
Does any particular incident or piece of work illustrate your child's difficulties or lack of progress?
Check as many of the points in your report as possible with your child and add their comments.

Extra points

If possible end your report with your answers to the following questions:
- Do you feel that your child's difficulties give 'significant' cause for concern or are 'severe and complex'? Often this means a child has much greater difficulties than others the same age and/or a child has considerable difficulties in more than one area, for example with hearing and behaviour.
- Do you feel that your child's needs have not been met, even though the school and experts have tried? Why do you feel this? Give details.
- Do you feel that your child may need the sort of help which normally only comes through a Statement? Why do you feel this? Give details.

Do not worry if you cannot answer any or all of these questions. End the report by signing and dating it. Make a copy and send it to the local authority with any reports that you feel are useful. Keep to the time limits given.

If you do not want to write a report, the local authority should arrange to meet you, write down what you say and then agree the wording with you, but it can be more difficult to make all your points this way.

If you need, or would prefer to have, an interpreter at any meetings about your child, the local authority should arrange one for you.

Chapter four
Making a Statement

Sometimes parents are so relieved when the local authority agrees to make a Statement that they feel their worries are over. As we keep reminding them in this handbook, however, it is important that the Statement identifies all their child's needs and matches those needs with detailed provision and at the end of this chapter we explain how to check the Statement for gaps, jargon and help which is too vague.

The law

If, following the assessment, the local authority decides that it should make or amend a Statement of special educational needs it has to follow detailed procedures on what must be included in any Statement (except for children aged under two for whom Statements can be made in any form). The law on the procedures for writing Statements is set out in **Schedule 27 of the Education Act 1996** and in the **Education (Special Educational Needs) (England) (Consolidation) Regulations 2001 (SI 3455)**and **(The Education (Special Educational Needs) (Wales) Regulations 2002 SI 152 (W20))** which we abbreviate here to **SEN Regs**.

Timetable for dealing with the proposed Statement

1. The local authority sends you a proposed Statement.
2. If you wish to express a preference for a school you must do so within 15 days of receiving the proposed Statement, or within 15 days of the date on which you last attended a meeting to discuss the contents of the pro-posed Statement.
3. If you wish to make representations to the local authority about the contents of the proposed Statement you have 15 days from the date of receiving the proposed Statement to do so, or 15 days from the date of any meeting with a local authority officer to discuss the proposed Statement. (See **Meeting a local authority officer** on page 58.)
4. If you wish to meet with a local authority officer to discuss the proposed Statement, you have 15 days to ask for the meeting from the date of receiving the proposed Statement.
5. If after such a meeting you still disagree with all or part of the proposed Statement, you have a further 15 days within which you can require further meetings to be arranged with the people responsible for providing advice, or someone else they suggest. The local authority can arrange more than one meeting if necessary if you disagree with more than one part of the advice.
6. Within eight weeks of issuing the proposed Statement (longer if your meetings extend this period) the local authority must issue a final Statement and begin making provision. You can appeal to the Tribunal (see Chapter 6) if you are unhappy with the final Statement.

The proposed Statement

Parents must be sent a copy of a proposed Statement or (following a reassess-ment) a proposed amended Statement along with copies of the advice the local authority was given, a list of all maintained primary or secondary schools and a list of non-maintained special schools and approved independent schools. The local authority will also send a letter with the proposed Statement. This will be long and detailed as it has to contain information that is required by law (SEN Reg 14). It should explain the opportunities parents have to express a preference for a school and to negotiate over the contents of the Statement (*see box*). It must also include contact details (**Part A Sched.1 SEN Regs**). This should all be sent to the parent within two weeks of completing the assessment.

All the reports and evidence gathered during statutory assessment should be with the Statement.

Statement format

Schedule 2 of the **SEN Regs** provides a model format for a Statement. The Statement should be clear about whether it is a proposed Statement, a final Statement or an amended Statement.

The Statement is made up of six parts:

Part 1: personal details

1. The child's name, address, date of birth, religion etc and contact details for the parent or carer.

2. List of the advice from parents and professionals which is attached in the appendices

Part 2: special educational needs

The local authority's view of the special educational needs of the child. All the learning difficulties identified in the advice collated in the appendices must be listed here – the SEN Toolkit suggests using the same headings as those used in the advice and recommends numbering each need so it can be easily matched with the corresponding provision.

Part 3: Special educational provision

1. Firstly, the objectives of the provision will be set out.

2. Secondly, the special educational provision which the authority considers appropriate to meet all the educational needs must be specified and normally quantified. This may include:

- facilities, therapy and equipment, staffing arrangements and curriculum.
- disapplications and modifications to the National Curriculum (including any arrangements for the national tests) together with details as to how a broad and balanced curriculum is to be maintained (**COP 8.38**). Where pupils are at the foundation stage, Part 3 should describe the help to enable the child to achieve the early learning goals. If the young person is about to take GCSEs or vocational examinations, the local authority should include any special examination provision recommended.
- where speech and language difficulties mean therapy is required, this must usually be specified in Part 3; only exceptionally will it appear in Part 6.
- where residential accommodation is appropriate.

The local authority should describe in Part 3 "all the mechanisms that will support the child". The SEN Toolkit lists the following provision which might be made:

- home-school liaison
- specialist teaching time
- specialist support and advice for the teaching staff
- staff supervision during break times
- access to specialist teaching programmes
- one-to-one small group work
- specialist equipment
- advice/support from external specialists
- small classes
- staff to pupil ratios
- staff who specialise in teaching pupils with particular needs
- residential provision

3. Thirdly, a description of monitoring arrangements to check whether progress is meeting the objectives. This should include:
- regular monitoring of progress in meeting objectives
- targets to meet the objectives and regular monitoring of these
- regular monitoring of any modifications to the National Curriculum
- regular monitoring of any provision substituted for the National Curriculum
- any special arrangements for reviewing the Statement
- arrangements and the timeframe for drawing up an Individual Education Plan. It should also include annual review arrangements, especially if the first review is to be held within a shorter period than a year.

Part 4: Placement
This part will remain blank on the proposed Statement. On the final statement local authorities must specify:
  a) the type and, normally, the name of a school or institution, or
  b) any provision made by the local authority under S19 EA96 for the child to be educated otherwise than at a school.

Part 5: Non-Educational Needs
Non-educational needs of the child may include medical needs, needs concerning mobility, respite care, specialist travel and health and safety.

Part 6: Non-Education Provision
Provision to meet the needs in Part 5 which would generally be made by education, health or social services. Local authorities should state the objectives to be achieved by the provision and describe any arrangements made with the body providing help. Part 6 has not the legal force of Part 3 and therefore the help in this part cannot be guaranteed.

Appendices
These set out all the representations, evidence, advice and information taken into account in making the Statement. Parental advice should include any representations made to the local authority when considering the need for assessment as well as their views and evidence submitted during the assessment.

ACE advice for local authorities
Where the advice in the appendices is conflicting or unclear, explain why you chose one view over another or give your reasons for the interpretation you have reached.

Drawing up the Statement

The Code gives local authorities advice on drafting Statements: *"LEAs should draft clear, unambiguous Statements. Where diagnostic or technical terms are necessary or helpful, for example in referring to specific disabilities, their meaning should be explained in terms that parents and other non-professionals will readily understand."* (COP 8.31)

Matching needs and provision

The Court of Appeal has taken a strong line about matching each identified educational need with provision. It said that this should be the case even if the school could make the provision without further help (R v Secretary of State for Education and Science, ex parte E 1992 [1 FLR 377]).

The Code reiterates this: *"A Statement should specify clearly the provision necessary to meet the needs of the child. It should detail appropriate provision to meet each identified need"* (COP 8.36).

The courts have also clarified the meaning of specifying provision in an important case known as L v Clarke and Somerset County Council 1997 [ELR 1998 129]. The case involved a boy with dyslexia whose Statement failed to set out the number of hours of help he should receive. His parents asked the High Court to consider whether the Tribunal were right not to order this. The judge said that *"... in very many cases it will not be possible to fulfil the requirement to specify the special educational provision considered appropriate to meet the child's needs, including specification of staffing arrangements and curriculum, unless hours per week are set out."*

He also said a Statement should be *"so specific and so clear as to leave no room for doubt as to what has been decided is necessary in the individual case."*

Although the judge did not go so far as to say all Statements must give this level of detail to comply with the law, he did imply that most must.

The Code points out that "Provision should normally be quantified (e.g. in terms of hours of provision, staffing arrangements)..." but adds that sometimes flexibility may be needed where a child has changing needs (COP 8.37).

The courts have also said that vague Statements which only describe provision in terms of a band, or cash figure or position on a matrix are unlawful. This local authority practice would not be enough to satisfy the requirement to specify provision in Part 3 of a Statement. The judge in one case (R v Cumbria County Council ex parte P 1994 [ELR 1995 337]) said that the appeal process would be impossible to operate if the parent did not know the nature of the provision that the authority intended to make.

Which Part?

As explained above, there is an important legal difference between Parts 2 and 3, which describe educational needs and provision and have the force of law, and Parts 5 and 6 which describe non-educational needs and provision and generally cannot be enforced. This point has particular importance in the case of support from social services which may be regarded as care, and therapies which may be regarded as medical provision. However, in both cases, there is often scope for arguing that there is an educational element and that therefore they should be recorded in Parts 2 and 3, instead of or as well as Parts 5 and 6.

The issue of whether different types of therapy are educational or not has been argued successfully on both sides and will often depend on the needs of the individual child.

Where the issue has been decided by Tribunal, the courts will generally accept their expert view. Depending on the individual circumstances, physiotherapy, occupational therapy and speech therapy could all be deemed to be educational (The Court of Appeal in the case of London Borough of Bromley v SENT 1998 [ELR 1999 260]).

Speech therapy

In the case of speech therapy there is now an understanding that this is an educational provision in almost all cases and therefore something which the local authority must make sure is provided.

Case law has established that speech and language therapy can be regarded as either educational or non-educational provision, or both, depending on the nature of the child's needs.

In the case known as the Lancashire Judgment (R v Lancashire CC, ex parte CM 1989), the court rejected the argument that because health authorities employed the speech therapists, speech therapy should appear in Parts 5 and 6 of a Statement rather than Parts 2 and 3. The court decided that to teach a child how to communicate by spoken language was just as much educational provision as to teach a child to communicate in writing.

The Code is also quite clear on the matter:

"...since communication is so fundamental in learning and progression, addressing speech and language impairment should normally be recorded as educational provision unless there are exceptional reasons for not doing so." (COP 8.49)

Although the Code points out that prime responsibility for speech and language therapy services rests with the NHS, it reminds local authorities that ultimate responsibility for ensuring that the provision is made rests with them unless parents make alternative arrangements (COP 8:51).

The courts backed this up in a case where, because of a lack of resources, a District Health Authority could only provide half the therapy needed by a child and specified in the Statement by the local authority. The local authority argued that its responsibility was to ask the health authority for help but the court said that merely asking for help did not relieve the local authority of its obligation to comply with the Statement. The court said that the obligation imposed on a local authority by S324 (5) EA96 to arrange the provision in a Statement is owed personally to the child and is non-delegable and is subject to no qualification, express or implied (R v London Borough of Harrow, ex parte M 1996 [ELR 1997 62]).

Types of school

Mainstream school – a school which is not a special school

Maintained school – a school funded by the local education authority

Maintained special school – a local authority-funded school which caters for the needs and education of children with a specific disability or combination of disabilities. Normally attended by pupils with Statements of special educational needs.

Non-maintained school – a non-profit-making special school approved under **S342 EA96** and which operates under the **Education (Special Educational Needs) (Approval of Independent School) Regulations 1994 [SI 651]**.

Independent school– a private school which, in this context, may receive approval under **S347 EA96** from the Secretary of State for the admission of children with Statements. Publicly funded schools, such as academies and city technology colleges, which are also regarded as independent do not require approval. (See page 18).

Naming a school
Mainstream places

Most children with Statements are taught in ordinary mainstream schools. The **SEN and Disability Discrimination Act 2001** gave parents a stronger right to a place in a mainstream school for their child when it required local authorities to educate a child with a Statement in a mainstream school where parents wished it and where it was not "incompatible with the provision of efficient education for other children. This Act amended **S316** of the **Education Act 1996 (S316 (3) EA96)** and means local authorities can only refuse mainstream education where the education of other children would suffer. *Inclusive Schooling* guidance says that 'other children' means only those children with whom the statemented child would be in direct daily contact. Schools and local authorities are expected to take reasonable steps to prevent any incompatability (S316A (6)). The guidance points out that "trivial and inappropriate reasons" should not be used to refuse a child a mainstream place and has warned that the Secretary of State will not hesitate to act if schools and local authorities behave unreasonably in this respect.

Unless parents ask for special school education, local authorities have a duty to educate in mainstream even when parents do not make a preference for an individual mainstream school. Only where there are no reasonable steps that can be taken by a school, local authority or another authority to prevent the incompatibility of a child's admission with the efficient education of other children, can the local authority refuse mainstream education. What constitutes reasonable steps depends on all of the circumstances of the individual case and the Government has said that it expects schools and local authorities to be increasingly able to meet the needs of children with a wide range of disabilities. The factors which local authorities might take into account when considering what is reasonable are:

a. would the steps be effective?

b. would they be practical?

c. what steps have already been taken to include the child, and have they worked?

d. are there any financial and other resources implications?

e. how disruptive would it be?

Inclusive Schooling and the *Code of Practice for schools on Part 4 of the Disability Discrimination Act 1995* give useful examples of reasonable steps which can be taken to include children in mainstream. The Code says that the duty to make reasonable adjustments assumes the involvement of disabled pupils in every aspect of school life.

Inclusive Schooling uses the example of behaviour difficulties to illustrate when it may not always be possible to include a child in mainstream. It highlights children's behaviour which:

● systematically, persistently and significantly threatens the safety of others; and

● systematically, persistently and significantly impedes the learning of others.

Other examples include constant attention seeking, which means that the teacher has to spend a greatly disproportionate amount of time with the child, and where there has been an extreme incident involving the child which is highly likely to recur. In both these examples there would still have to be consideration of whether there were reasonable steps that could be taken to prevent the child's behaviour affecting other pupils. For example, could employing an LSA to support the child enable the teacher to give attention to the whole class?

"It is reasonable to expect a local education authority to be able to provide a mainstream education for nearly all children with special educational needs. However, it is not reasonable or practical to expect all schools to provide for every possible type of special educational need" (Inclusive Schooling: par 29).

Parents' right to state a preference for a maintained school

When parents are sent the proposed Statement or proposed amended Statement, the local authority will ask if they wish to express a preference for a particular maintained (i.e. local authority funded) school. The proposed (or proposed amended) Statement must be accompanied by lists of different types of schools in the area (*see* **The proposed Statement** *page 44*) and parents should be informed that the parent partnership service is able to provide information about schools (**SEN Reg 14** and **Part A, Sched.1 SEN Regs 2001**).

In the final Statement, Part 4 will set out the type of school and any particular school which the local authority considers appropriate for the child, or any arrangements for provision of education otherwise than at school (*see page 56*). But this part must be left blank when the proposed Statement is issued, so that the local authority does not pre-empt the parents' right to state a preference for a maintained school, or make representations for a non-maintained special or independent school **(COP 8.42)**.

The strengthened right to a mainstream place does not mean that parents have an unqualified right to a place at a particular mainstream school for their child; nor does it prevent them stating a preference for a maintained special school.

The law which deals with parental preference is found in **Schedule 27** of the **Education Act 1996**. This says that the local authority must name the maintained school that parents prefer unless:

● the school is unsuitable for the child's age, ability and aptitude and the special educational needs set out in Part 2 of the Statement, or

● the child's attendance is incompatible with the efficient education of other children in the school or the efficient use of the local authority's resources. **(Sched.27 EA96)**

The courts have examined the interaction between **Schedule 27** (parental preference) and **S316** and **316A** of the **EA96** (presumption in favour of mainstream schooling). The most recent case involved a mother who appealed against Hounslow LEA's refusal to name the school of her choice. The High Court gave guidance on how local authorities should proceed with naming a school which would have resulted in each school being examined under the conditions set out under **Schedule 27** without **S316** ever coming into play – in effect undermining the intention of Parliament to provide mainstream schooling for most children whose parents wished it.

The mother appealed and the Court of Appeal said that the process for considering parental preference under **Schedule 27** was entirely distinct both in nature and purpose from the process whereby a local authority discharged its duty under **S316** and **S316A**. The starting point for the local authority would be the parents' preference. Only if the local authority decided against their preference on the basis of the grounds listed above would S316A(4) (i.e. duty to provide mainstream education) come into operation. The court also concluded that S316 did not impose a positive duty on the local authority to name a particular school in the Statement (as opposed to just a type of school) although normally this would be the case. (R (on the application of MH) v (1) SENDIST (2) Hounslow London Borough 2004 [ELR 2004 424]).

Is the school suitable?

Once parents have expressed a preference for a school a local authority will consider the individual school's suitability for the child. Clearly the local authority is unlikely to name a secondary school for a child of primary school age or a selective school if the child does not meet the criteria for selection. In many cases, however, suitability will hinge on the school's facilities to meet that child's particular disability or special educational needs. So if the child needed a mainstream school adapted for a wheelchair, the local authority is unlikely to name a school on three floors with no lift, even if the parents prefer it, if there is a mainstream school already adapted in the area. They could argue that the school is unsuitable.

Sometimes parents will state a preference for a special school or indicate that they would like special school education. The local authority is then under no over-riding duty to educate in mainstream. If, however, it feels that a special school is not suitable for the child, it may name a mainstream school with appropriate support.

Local authorities must have regard to parents' views about a child's religion and identity when deciding a child's special educational needs and the required provision. They would have to consider if the views were relevant to those needs and the manner in which they might be met. In the case of a seven-year-old Jewish girl with cerebral palsy, a decision of the Special Educational Needs and Disability Tribunal was quashed because it failed to take proper account of the impact of a child's Jewishness in assessing her special educational needs and the provision to be made for them (A v SENDIST & LB Barnet 2003 [ELR 2004 293]).

Local authority consultation

The local authority must consult the governing body of the parents' preferred school and, if the school is in another local authority area, that local authority as well, sending full details of the child's special educational needs and provision. The local authority has the final decision on which school to name in the Statement but it will take the views of the governing body into account. If a maintained school is named on a Statement the school must admit the child. If the local authority decides, for one of the reasons allowed in Schedule 27 (*see above*) not to name the parent's preferred school, it will identify another maintained school and consult in the same way (Par 3, Sched. 27 EA96).

When a local authority proposes to name an academy in a Statement, the academy "*shall consent to being named, except where admitting the child would be incompatible with the provision of efficient education for other children and where no reasonable steps may be made to secure compatibility*" (Annex 3 of the academy funding agreement with government).

If an academy does not consent to be named on a Statement of SEN on these grounds, and the local authority disagrees, the local authority may not name the academy regardless. A new mediation service has been set up for authorities and academies. Parents, it appears, will not be included. If no agreement is reached between the academy and the authority, the academy may refer the case to the Secretary of State to make a determination. The government regards academies as *"fully inclusive schools and therefore must admit pupils with SEN on an equal basis with others and that this should be reflected in their admissions policy"*.

Efficient education and the efficient use of resources

The issues of a child's admission being incompatible with efficient education or efficient use of resources might arise where a school is full – i.e. it has reached its admissions number for that year group. These numbers indicate the minimum number of children a school must admit and the local authority will have to consider the difficulties that an additional child might make to the school. A total number for the whole school, rather than each year group, is fixed for special schools. In their case the Code advises that local authorities consider the number in the class to which the child would be admitted rather than the total for the whole school.

Local authorities must comply with legislation which limits infant class sizes to 30 pupils although the legislation allows the entry of an additional child where not to admit them would be "prejudicial to his or her interests". These excepted pupils can include a child who receives a Statement naming the school or where a child with a Statement naming the school moves into the area. In either case this only applies where an admission is outside the normal admissions round; the class can only remain at above 30 for the remainder of that school year. **The Education (England) (Infant Class Sizes) Regs 1998 [SI 1973]** and **(The Education (Wales) (Infant Class Sizes) Regs 1998 [SI 1943]**

The Code of Practice on Admissions also allows for children attending mainstream infant classes who would normally be educated in a special school or a SEN unit attached to a mainstream school to be treated as excepted pupils for any time they spend in the infant class. This is in recognition of such arrangements, including dual placements, which are encouraged as a way of supporting inclusion. For placements to be deemed mainstream, pupils must spend the majority of their time (i.e. 51% or more) at a mainstream school.

Resources may be used as a reason for refusing parents' preference for a particular school, but may not be used to deny a child a place in mainstream.

If the decision is between special schools in different boroughs the resources to be taken into account are those of the local authority with responsibility for making the Statement, rather than the resources of the public purse (B v. London Borough of Harrow, the House of Lords 1999 [ELR 2000 109]). Parents, therefore, cannot rely on the fact that a special school place in another local authority would cost no more than a special school place in their own authority. If there is a vacancy in a local maintained special school, the local authority will want to fill that funded place before paying for an out of borough placement because it will already be funding their own school up to their approved number.

Another Court of Appeal case against a Tribunal decision in favour of a parent who wanted the Statement to name an independent school rather than a maintained school went further. It held that a straight comparison of cost was not the right way to evaluate "unreasonable public expenditure" (**S9 EA96**: *see below*). The Tribunal should have taken into account that the local authority

would incur the cost of a specialist teacher at the maintained school and transport costs whether or not the child attended (Oxfordshire CC v GB and Others
2001 [ELR 2002 8]).

Independent and non–maintained special schools
Making representations

Sometimes parents feel that only a particular non-maintained special school
(schools often run by voluntary organisations) or an independent school can
meet their child's needs. Although parents have no right to "state a preference"
for such a school they may "make representations". The difference being that
the local authority does not have a qualified duty to comply with their choice.
We describe that qualified duty under the heading **Parents' right to state a
preference** (*above*). The local authority must, however, have regard to the general principle in law (**S9 EA96**) that "pupils are to be educated in accordance
with the wishes of their parents, so far as that is compatible with the provision
of efficient instruction and training and the avoidance of unreasonable public
expenditure", and its duty to arrange suitable special education (**S324 EA96**)

In practice this means that, while the local authority will listen to parents'
views, the starting point for them will be whether there is suitable provision
within the maintained sector. It is not enough for parents to argue that an independent school has good facilities and would therefore be best for their child.
They would have to show that local authority provision was unable to meet
their child's needs.

If the local authority and the parents agree that the child should be placed in
an independent school which is not approved by the Secretary of State under
S347 EA96, the local authority must seek the Secretary of State's consent to
the placement before naming the school in the final copy of the Statement. The
Secretary of State may have a policy about such consent but must look at each
case on its merits (R v Secretary of State for Education and Employment ex
parte P 2000 [ELR 2000 300]). Academies and city colleges are exempt from
this requirement.

Before naming an independent school (including academies and city colleges) or a non-maintained special school in a Statement, the local authority
should consult the school.

Parents may also make representations for their child to attend an establishment outside England and Wales. While this is rare, local authorities may contribute to or pay the fees of the institution and travelling expenses.

If the local authority does not agree to the parents' representations, it should
inform them of its decision before it names any other school in the final
Statement. This is to give parents the opportunity to state a preference for a
particular maintained school if they wish to. Alternatively parents can appeal
against the local authority decision to the Tribunal.

Parents may choose to send their child to a fee-paying independent school
at their own expense. If the child has a Statement the local authority must be
satisfied that the school can make the provision to meet the child's needs; otherwise they must name another school. If the local authority is satisfied that
the child's parents have made suitable arrangements, and that there is a realistic possibility of them being funded for a reasonable period, it must state the
type of provision in Part 4 of the child's Statement but it is not required to

specify the name of a school. The local authority is still under a duty to maintain the child's Statement and to review it annually (S324 (4) EA96) (COP 8.97). The issue of whether a local authority should contribute towards the additional help a child needs in a private school has been the subject of a number of legal wrangles, for example in the case of Aladay v Richmond 2004 where the court held that the parents could not compel the local authority to meet the additional costs of the child's special educational provision as set out in the child's Statement. Local authorities may decide to pay such costs, and sometimes do, but presumably need to be convinced that they can justify the expense in the context of their stewardship of public funds.

A parent can make representations for an academy to be named in a Statement (S9 EA96 and *Inclusive Schooling, para 31*). However, an academy can refuse to admit a child with a Statement even if the local authority judges it to be the most suitable. The final decision rests with the Secretary of State. If the academy agrees to take a child but the local authority names another school, parents can appeal to SENDIST.

Residential placements

Where a residential school is being considered, the local authority should look at the child's circumstances in the context of policies about residential placements drawn up with social services.

Parents seeking a boarding school may need to argue that only a residential placement can meet their child's *educational* needs. The issue of whether a child's needs are educational was the focus of a parental appeal against a Tribunal decision not to name a residential shool for an autistic boy (W v Leeds CC and SENDIST 2004 [ELR 2005 459]. The court accepted that the child may have a need for constant supervision but rejected the parent's argument that this was an educational need, at least outside normal school hours. Although the Tribunal had agreed that there needed to be an interagency approach, it felt it was not the responsibility of the education authority to pay for care in the absence of social services funding.

If care for a child is needed, parents could ask social services to contribute towards this but there is no Tribunal appeal if they refuse. The courts have reached different decisions about whether social services' funds should be taken into account when comparing costs of one placement with another. It will be interesting to see whether the emphasis on integrated services for children under the Children Act 2004 will make joint funding arrangements easier. The Code says that residential provision is likely to be considered where the child:

1. has severe or multiple SEN that cannot be met in local day provision

2. has severe or multiple special educational needs that require a consistent programme both during and after school hours that cannot be provided by parents with support from other agencies

3. is looked after by the local authority and has complex social and learning needs, and the placement is joint-funded with social services

4. has complex medical needs as well as learning needs that cannot be managed in local day provision and the placement is joint-funded with the health authority.

The Code recommends that in these circumstances a multi-agency plan should be put into place that enables tripartite funding.

When parents and the local authority agree that a residential school should be named in the child's Statement, the local authority should also agree arrangements for the child's contact with their family and for any special help, such as transport, which may be needed to maintain home/school contact (COP 8.70).

Parents' participation in assessments and reviews when a child is away from home is particularly important, says the Code (COP 2.9). It recommends parents visit the school proposed by the local authority to enable them to discuss their child's special needs with the headteacher, SENCO or any specialist teaching staff. *"Every effort should be made to provide any additional information and advice or to arrange any further visits which will help them reach an informed decision about their child's future".* (COP 8.78)

If parents do not want a residential placement local authorities will generally try to find an alternative placement nearer to home. However it is likely to depend on the facts of the case as two High Court cases demonstrate. In one case CB v Merton London Borough Council and the Special Educational Needs Tribunal 2002 [ELR 2002 441] the High Court agreed with the Tribunal that there was no suitable school nearer to home. The court found that although the decision might interfere with the right to a family life (**Article 8** of the **Human Rights Act 1998**) the interference was justified under the Act (**Article 8 (2)**). In the case of R (M) v Worcestershire CC 2004 [ELR 2005 48] the court accepted that a residential school would not be appropriate if the parents opposed the placement.

Where a child is placed in a residential school with the intention that it will be for longer than three months, the local authority must inform social services either in the area where the child's family live or in the area of the residential school. It is good practice to inform both (**S85 Children Act 1989**).

If a child is in public care social services must, where practicable, consult the local authority before placing the child in a residential school. Where they have already placed a child in such a school, they must as soon as possible inform the local authority of the arrangements that have been made for the child's accommodation (**S28 Children Act 1989**).

Education otherwise than at school

Children with Statements but not in school are described as being "educated otherwise than at school". This happens when the local authority has made other arrangements, for example in a pupil referral unit, home tuition, or various types of provision permitted for Key Stage 4 pupils. It can also happen if parents decide to home educate their child.

If a home-educated child has a Statement, the local authority still has a duty to ensure that the child's needs are met. Only if the local authority is satisfied that the child is receiving a suitable education is it relieved of the duty to make the provision specified in the Statement.

The local authority need not name a school in Part 4 of the Statement when a child is being home educated but the Code recommends that Part 4 states the type of school the local authority considers appropriate. In these circumstances the Code recommends the following wording for Part 4 : *"Parents have made their own arrangements under S7 of the Education Act 1996".* (**S7** requires parents to secure full-time education for their child suitable to their age, ability and aptitude, and any special educational needs they may have.) The Statement can also specify any provision that the local authority have agreed to make to help parents provide suitable education for their child at home.

If the parents of a child with a Statement want their child to leave the school which is named in the Statement and to educate them at home instead, they have a similar duty as other home educating parents. They must provide an education which is suitable but in addition the education must also meet their child's special educational needs. Before a child is removed from the school which is named on the Statement, the Code advises parents to inform the local authority of their intention and to ask for the Statement to be amended so that it no longer names a school. Parents can withdraw their child from a mainstream school which is named in a Statement and should inform the school that they want the child's name removed from the admission register. This is important if they are not to risk proceedings for their child's non-attendance. However, if the Statement names a special school which has been arranged for the child by the local authority, a child's name may not be removed from the register without the consent of the local authority. If this is refused, parents can apply to the Secretary of State for a direction that the child's name be removed from the register. (**Education (Pupil Registration) Regulations 1995 [SI 2089]**. (*See* **Attendance** *page 103*) Local authorities may suggest home education but they cannot require parents to make special educational provision for their own child (DM and KC v Essex County Council and SENDIST 2003 [ELR 2003 419]).

Social services placements

Where education for a child with a Statement is provided by social services, for example in a children's home, the local authority has the status of corporate parent. The LA must consider whether it has made suitable provision (S324 (5)(a)). If it is satisfied with the arrangements it need not name a school in Part 4 of the Statement but it must name the type of provision.

Non-educational needs and provision

Parts 5 and 6 of a Statement describe the child's non-educational needs and matching provision. Part 6 should also state the objectives to be achieved by the provision and set out any arrangements for its delivery agreed by the local authority with other agencies. Parents should know that whilst Parts 3, and 4 of the Statement are legally binding on the local authority, Parts 5 and 6 are not and there is no right of appeal to the Tribunal about these. Local authorities should explain this important point to parents (**COP 8.47**).

Final Statement

The local authority must send a copy of the final Statement to the child's parents and give written notice of their rights of appeal to the Tribunal and the time limits for lodging an appeal – within two months of receiving the local authority's decision (see pages 81-82). They should also tell parents of parent partnership and disagreement resolution services, and the fact that the parent's right of appeal is not affected by taking part in disagreement resolution. When changes are to the proposed Statement are agreed by the LA and the parents, the final Statement should be issued immediately. Local authorities must arrange the educational provision from the date which the Statement is made.

Meeting a local authority officer

Remember, you do not have unlimited time to ask for changes to the proposed Statement so act quickly:

- record the date you received the draft as your first 15 day period to submit your views starts on that date; remember you can 'stop the clock' by asking for a meeting or an extension;
- if your first language is not English and you find the proposed Statement difficult to understand, ask the local authority for help with translation
- if someone is helping or advising you, give them a copy of the whole Statement and the appendices immediately
- explain the Statement to your child and note any comments
- check there are copies of all the reports which the local authority has received from professionals who have examined your child along with any other advice (including anything submitted by you) which they have taken into account in making the Statement. If you believe something is missing, ask about it immediately
- now start going through the various parts of the Statement in detail. Use photocopies so that you can make notes on one copy while keeping a clean one.

When you meet a local authority officer to discuss the proposed Statement, be clear about what you want to discuss. You will need to explain your concerns and your reasons and seek any further information. Make a list of all the points you wish to make and don't feel embarrassed about taking it with you. Follow **Examining a Proposed Statement in Detail** (see opposite page) to help you identify all the issues you wish to raise at the meeting.

At the meeting it is best to start with the points on which you are most likely to reach agreement. As you finish each issue note where you and the local authority officer have agreed or disagreed. Check that this is also his or her understanding. If you have the confidence, ask them to sign your notes at the end of the meeting.

After this meeting you have 15 days to seek further meetings with anyone who provided the local authority with advice for the Statement. You might want to ask them to expand on their advice or be more specific about the help that your child needs.

If you do not feel confident about presenting your case on your own, ask your Independent Parental Supporter, a friend or representative to go with you.

Making your final comments

After the last of these meetings, you have a final period of 15 days in which to submit your comments on anything in the Statement with which you still disagree. In drafting these comments, keep your objective – the school and provision which you believe will best meet your child's needs in mind. Your comments could cover:

1. the actual wording you would like to see in the section
2. your reasons for any proposals
3. details of anything in the advisers' reports, from other assessments you have acquired, from local authority policies etc. which support your proposals.

Examining the proposed Statement in detail

You will need a spare copy of the Statement and the advice reports, paper and pen and felt tips.

Check Part 2 of the Statement

Is the Statement clear about all your child's difficulties and the exact help they need? For example, would a new teacher reading it for the first time be able to work out your child's main learning difficulties?

Underline anything which is unclear.

The proposed Statement will be attached to all the advice reports on your child. These may be listed as appendices. Check that all the reports listed are there. Go through them with a coloured felt tip pen or highlighter. Highlight each difficulty or 'need' described in them. Check that Part 2 of the Statement lists all these difficulties. Tick them off one by one. If any are missing or seem different from those in the report, make a note.

Do any of the experts who wrote about your child disagree? Is there anything you do not understand? Underline the points where this is the case.

Is the Statement clear about which difficulties are most serious or does it look as though they are all of equal importance? You could make a list of the difficulties in order of importance.

Now, make a note of any disagreements or gaps, and list anything which is unclear.

Check Part 3 of the Statement

Now go to Part 3 where the help for your child is described. Look under Part 3(b), the provision section.

Does the help match the needs?

Is there help for every difficulty listed in Part 2 and in the reports? Do they match? Make a note of any gaps.

Go back to the advice reports and highlight with a different coloured felt tip any help they recommend. Now check that the help is in Part 3. Make a note of any gaps. If there is anything you do not understand, underline it and make a note.

Is there enough help?

Reports from different professionals may disagree about the help needed or they may leave out the help altogether. If there are gaps or disagreements, make a note. If you disagree with any of the views on your child's needs or help, also make a note.

Is the help described in detail?

Sometimes Statements can be vague or hard to understand.

To be clear about what your child's help will amount to on a typical day at school, ask yourself the following:

- What type of help my child will get? e.g. equipment, learning support, teaching programme, speech therapy, behaviour support.
- Who will give the help?
- Do they need particular qualifications or experience?
- How many hours of extra help are there?
- How often will the help happen?
- What teaching strategies will staff use?
- Will teaching be one to one or in small groups?
- If teaching is in groups, how big will they be?
- How will they know if the help is working?

ACE advice for IPSs

If you are helping someone who has difficulty with English, remember that the Code says local authorities should seek advice from bilingual support staff, teachers of English as an additional language, interpreters and translators and other local sources of help to ensure parents and children are fully involved.

- How often will they check progress?
- How will I be involved?

Make a note of any gaps, anything that is unclear or anything you do not agree with or understand.

Now ask what will happen when something different happens at school e.g. if the usual teacher is away or if a trips is planned. Does the Statement include the extra help your child may need to spend nights away from home? If your child's condition or disability means they have days when they have more problems than others, does the Statement include sufficient help for the 'bad' days? Finally, check that break times and lunch breaks are covered if your child needs help during these periods.

Now take a look at your list of points. If you think the help is not right or not clear enough, or if you have a lot of questions, you can ask to meet with the Named Officer at the local authority. If you have questions about one of the reports written by a professional, you can ask for a meeting with them.

Which school?

Deciding which school you feel would be right for your child can be difficult for all parents. When the decision may include choosing between mainstream or special, a unit in a mainstream school or a mixture of special and mainstream, parents may feel they need some help. The Code says that parents should be supported in making choices (**COP 8.68**) and parent partnership schemes should provide information in a range of appropriate languages and in a variety of mediums. The proposed Statement must be accompanied by lists of maintained and independent schools. An Independent Parental Supporter or a friend may accompany you on any school visits you wish to make. When you phone to arrange a visit, ask for copies of the school's SEN policy and disability accessibility plan, behaviour policy and the school prospectus. You could also ask for any recent Ofsted inspection reports. These are available from the school, local libraries or the Ofsted website: www.ofsted.gov.uk

You need to remember, however, that although the law says that the school named in the Statement must be suitable, this does not mean the local authority has to choose the 'best' provision for your child. The word 'choice' may also be misleading – you have a right to state a preference which the local authority has a duty to comply with- unless certain circumstances apply (see page 51). Below we provide some questions to help you decide which school is right:

Start with your child

What is your child good at?
What does your child like to do?
Any health problems now or in the early years?
Any social problems – shyness, victim of bullying?
Any family problems?
Any emotional problems – anxiety, tantrums?
Any problems at school?
Have any recent changes affected your child?

Are there any questions you want to ask about how your child would fit the school?

Questions to ask all schools

Do staff have appropriate skills and access to training to help my child?
What experience do they have of children with similar disabilities to my child?
Are there any specialist resources?
Is the building accessible?
Is the curriculum accessible?
How big are the classes?
Will my child's support be from the same people?
How will they receive information about my child?
What is the best way for parents to communicate with the school?
What arrangements are there when specialist teachers/helpers are ill?
Will my child have access to appropriate therapy?
Will there be any help with daily living skills?
What arrangements are there for giving medicines?
How many children with Statements have been excluded in the last two or three years?

Mainstream or special?

Most children with Statements of SEN are educated in mainstream schools. There has been some movement in recent years towards 'inclusion' – where children with disabilities attend ordinary schools but many children – around a third of those with Statements – are educated in special schools. Those arguing for inclusion say that children should not be segregated because of disability; they should have the same social and curriculum opportunities as non-disabled pupils and should not be isolated from their neighbourhoods and have to endure long journeys to schools which are often far from their homes.

Mainstream schools

Questions parents could ask mainstream schools include:
What are the school's targets for children with SEN?
Will my child be fully included in all school activities including those taking place out of school? Are playtimes and lunchtimes covered? Should the Statement include extra support for these?
How does the school try to prevent bullying of children with SEN? Do pupils receive disability awareness training?
Do the behaviour policies recognise that some children with special educational needs may need extra support to follow rules?

Special schools

Some parents and professionals believe that special schools are best for some children. They argue that there is greater expertise in educating children with disabilities, better access to specialist equipment and treatment and smaller classes. Often parents feel staff are more accepting of their child's difficulties and there is less risk of bullying, although this is not necessarily the case.

- the Ombudsman investigating maladministration
- Ofsted inspection teams
- the Connexions service for the purposes of writing or amending a Transition Plan
- a young offender institution carrying out duties under rule 38 of the Young Offender Institution Rules 2000
- an education researcher who the local authority believes may advance the education of children with SEN (but access will be conditional on researchers not publishing anything from the Statement which would identify the child or parents).

(SEN Reg 24)

Annual reviews

A local authority must review a Statement at least every 12 months. Parents must be fully involved in the annual review process and must be invited to the review meeting convened by the headteacher. The meeting is often described as the annual review, but the review is in four parts:

1. information gathering by the head
2. annual review meeting
3. head's report of the meeting to the local authority
4. local authority decision, in the light of the report, about whether to amend the Statement, cease to maintain it or continue to maintain it unchanged.

Aims

The annual review gathers together information for the school and other professionals planning the child's support. It should aim:

- to assess the child's progress in relation to the objectives specified in the Statement
- to review the application of the provisions of the National Curriculum to the child and the progress made in relation to those provisions
- to review the special provision including any special arrangements made because of modification or disapplication of the National Curriculum
- to review any progress made by the child in his behaviour and attitude to learning
- to consider whether the Statement continues to be appropriate – for example, have the child's needs changed or should provision be changed? The review should consider whether any amendments would be appropriate and whether the authority should cease to maintain the Statement
- to set new targets for the coming year to be reviewed at the next annual review.

(SEN Regs 20)

Timing

Local authorities must review a Statement (except for children under two) within 12 months of making it, and then within every 12 months after that (S328 EA96). Reviews may take place more frequently. For very young children under five whose rapid development can mean correspondingly rapid changes in needs, local authorities should consider reviewing the Statement at least every six months to ensure the help still meets the child's needs. However old the child, the timing should reflect their individual circumstances, for example, the date may need to be adjusted when a move to secondary school is imminent (*see below*).

When a Statement is amended following an annual review, the date of the next annual review should continue to be determined according to the date on which the Statement was made or reviewed rather than the date on which it was amended. When a second or subsequent statutory assessment results in a new Statement then the review should be within 12 months of the date of the new Statement (S328 EA96 and COP 9.2).

Interim reviews

It is open to local authorities and schools to bring forward an annual review or for parents to ask for an early review. This might be because of a sudden deterioration in a child's health or development, a change to their circumstances such as a new diagnosis or a crisis in which their needs are shown to be much greater than previously recognised. Such a review may be called an interim review, an interim annual review or just an early annual review.

Interim reviews are described in several areas of government guidance:

1. Exclusions

An interim review may be needed where a school identifies a pupil with a Statement as being at serious risk of disaffection or exclusion. Calling an early review to consider the pupil's changing needs is recommended as an alternative to exclusion (COP 9.44). This is also supported by the *SEN Toolkit (Paragraph 2, Section 9)* which says that an interim or early review should be called to consider the pupil's changing needs and recommend amendments to the Statement as an alternative to exclusion. The government's exclusions guidance: (*Paragraphs 43 and 44) Improving Behaviour and Attendance (2004)* reiterates the importance of liaising with the local authority and calling an interim review well before a pupil's behaviour escalates to the point of exclusion. If a child is permanently excluded the headteacher is expected to work with the local authority to see whether more support can be made available or whether a new school is an option. Where this can be arranged before the governors meet to review the exclusion, the head should normally withdraw the exclusion.

2. Changing needs

The SEN Toolkit recognises that interim reviews may be needed when a child has needs that are known to change rapidly (*Paragraph 3, Section 9*)

3. School transfer

The Code suggests another situation where an interim review might be needed. This is when it is unclear at the Year 5 review which school a child will move on to at secondary stage, the Code suggests that in interim review may be needed to comply with the requirement to amend the Statement by February 15 of the year of transfer to name the new school. (*See below.*)

4. Disagreements

The SEN Toolkit also suggests interim reviews where there is a disagreement at the review meeting over a particular course of action. It suggests that reviewing that action over a shorter period might be one way of resolving the dispute (*Paragraph 3, Section 9*).

ACE advice for parents

If you have comments about any of the written advice put them in writing and send them to the headteacher as soon as possible. Ask for help from support organisations to comment on reports or draw up your own advice if necessary.

Parents' checklist

You should be fully included in the annual review process. You will be sent:

● a letter from the school inviting you to provide written advice for the review and inviting you to the review meeting. You should be told that you can bring a friend, relative or adviser to the meeting.
● copies of all the advice contributing to the review at least two weeks before the meeting.
● a copy of the report the head makes to the local authority.

The revue process and timetable

1. Within two weeks of the start of each term the local authority must write to remind headteachers of all pupils for whom the authority maintains Statements and who will require an annual review that term (**SEN Reg 18**). Health and social services must also be notified. If the head requests advice, generally these services must respond (**S322(1) EA96** and **COP 9.15**).
2. The head must request written advice about the child's progress and the appropriateness of the Statement from:
   ● parents/carers
   ● anyone whom the local authority specifies
   ● anyone the head thinks appropriate.
   (**SEN Reg 20(4)**)

The head must arrange a meeting for each pupil needing an annual review and invite:
   ● the child's parent/carer
   ● members of staff whom the head thinks have appropriate knowledge
   ● the representative of the local authority which maintains the Statement
   ● anyone the local authority specifies in the notice sent to the head.
   (**SEN Reg 20(6)**)

3. At least two weeks before the review meeting the head must circulate copies of any written advice, inviting comments, to anyone who has not said they will not be attending (**SEN Reg 20(7)**).
4. No later than ten school days after the annual review meeting or the end of that school term – whichever is the earlier – the head must send a report to the local authority, and copies to everyone concerned with the review including parents (**SEN Regs 18(4)** and **20(12)**).

The report will summarise the meeting's conclusions and include the head's assessment of the main issues discussed, recommendations about any educational targets for the coming year and any recommendations, with their reasons, about whether the Statement should be amended or maintained (**COP 9.32**). (Arrangements for the review meetings for pupils in Year 9 and beyond follow similar procedures but with some important differences. These are dealt with at the end of the chapter.)

5. The final part of the review process is when the local authority decides whether to accept the headteacher's recommendations. In particular the local authority must decide whether to amend or cease to maintain the Statement and, within one week of making a decision, must send a copy of its decision to the headteacher, the child's parents and anyone else they think appropriate.

The review meeting

As well as the written advice and the points listed under Aims (*above*) the meeting must consider any significant changes in the child's circumstances during the year. A review meeting may make recommendations which will be included in the headteacher's report to the local authority. The Code says amendments to the Statement are likely to be recommended if:
   ● significant new evidence has emerged which is not recorded on the Statement
   ● significant needs recorded on the Statement are no longer present

- the provision needs to be changed to meet the child's changing needs and new targets
- the child should change school.

If parents disagree with the recommendations from the meeting or wish to add further information or views, they could follow up the review meeting by sending their own report to the local authority, perhaps requesting an amendment. The head's report should say if there were different recommendations but there is no reason why they should not write to give fuller reasons if they wish.

If parents are unhappy with the outcome of the review, they should ask the SENCO to keep in close touch with them over their child's progress. If there are plans to amend the Statement or cease to maintain it, they have the right of appeal. In some circumstances, for example if a local authority decides against amending a Statement even though this is recommended (*see below*), they may need to ask the local authority to undertake a reassessment of their child.

Parents' involvement

One of the Code's key principles is working in partnership with parents and it points out that acknowledging and drawing on parental knowledge and expertise in relation to their child is a good foundation for this (**COP 2.7**). Parents must be asked for their advice in relation to their child's progress and should be offered help by the head where they need it to write their advice. The school can either help the parent directly or suggest they contact the parent partnership service or the local authority Named Officer.

The Code points out that schools need to recognise the need for flexibility in the timing and structure of meetings to ensure parents can attend. Parents should be provided with documents well in advance of the review meeting. Special arrangements may need to be made for families with English as an additional language or where the child or family have other communication difficulties. The SEN Toolkit says that parents should be told that they can bring a friend, relative or adviser to the review meeting (*Paragraph 11, Section 9*). All parents should be encouraged to contribute to discussions about any proposals for new targets for their child's progress. If a parent fails to attend or contribute, the Code says this should be recorded in the review report with any reasons given.

Professionals are often unable to attend meetings so if parents want to discuss issues raised in the reports of professionals who do not attend, they should be advised at the review meeting to approach the named local authority officer either at the meeting or later if they do not attend.

Pupils' involvement

"From an early age, children with SEN should be actively involved at an appropriate level in discussions about their IEPs, including target setting and review arrangements and have their views recorded" (**COP 3:9**).

The review is also a good opportunity for pupil participation which, the Code says, should be the goal for all children. It stresses the need for active involvement as a way of improving the self confidence of young people with SEN. The involvement should be progressive so that by Year 9 when the Transition Plan (*see below*) is prepared, young people should be taking part in the review meeting where they wish this. The Code suggests local pupil support or advocacy

ACE advice for parents

If a new proposal such as a change of school is made without warning at the meeting you should consider asking for an adjournment.

ACE advice for schools

If the statemented child is also 'looked after' by the local authority make sure that the young person's social worker is invited to the annual review. Depending on the child's circumstances, parents and carers may also need to be invited. See **Who does what: How social workers and carers can support the education of looked after children** 2004, DfES.

services, often developed in partnership with health and social services, could support the young person, particularly when the young person is in public care although it warns that there needs to be clarity about the role of social worker or carer.

Advice on pupil participation is included in the *SEN Toolkit* which provides good practice information for schools and local authorities. It points out that children should be allowed a friend or ally with them at meetings but that choice must be theirs. Children with particular needs may require special help to communicate their views. The head should make sure they are properly prepared for meetings and have time to think about what they want to say and have the chance to ask questions.

Guidance on measuring the progress of pupils with severe learning difficulties (*Supporting the Target Setting Process, DfEE, 2001*]) describes ways of communicating with pupils which are relevant to involving pupils in the annual review. For example, facial expressions, gestures and eye contact may be recorded as well as conventional written and spoken communication. Similar useful advice is available in the Welsh Assembly guidance: *Section 3 Pupil Participation of The Handbook of Good Practice for Children with SEN.*

Children educated out of school

Children educated otherwise than at school – in hospitals, pupil referral units or at home, for example, will still have their Statements reviewed but the local authority is responsible for convening the review meeting and must invite the child's parents. The views of the designated medical officer for SEN should be sought where a child has major health problems and professional advisers from the relevant child health services should be invited to the meeting.

Amending the Statement following a review

If the local authority decides to amend the Statement, it should do it without delay. The **SEN Regulations (Reg 20(14)** stipulate that within one week of completing the review the authority must send copies of their decisions and recommendations to parents, the headteacher and any other appropriate person. The authority must inform parents of their right to make representations about the Statement and the amendments within 15 days and their right to request a meeting with an officer. It must explain the reasons and ensure parents have copies of any evidence that prompted the proposal. It must also send parents a copy of the existing Statement (**Par. 2A(4) Sched.27 EA96 amended**). The local authority proposals should be appended to the Notice to Parents set out in the Regulations (**Part B, Sched. 1, Annex A).**

Parents' rights

Parents must be told of their right of appeal and their right to express a preference for a maintained school or make representations for another type of school where the proposal involves amending Part 4 of the Statement. Parents should be sent lists of maintained schools and any lists of non-maintained special schools and approved independent schools issued by the Secretary of State and the National Assembly of Wales.

Whether or not parents would like to change their child's school, this is an important opportunity for them to negotiate changes to the Statement. Parents' representations are not restricted to the amendments suggested by the local authority, they can request changes to any aspect of the Statement and the local authority must consider them before deciding whether and how to amend the Statement. So if, for example, the local authority is proposing to amend the Statement because a child is about to transfer to secondary school, parents may request that other parts of the Statement also be amended to reflect the different circumstances. When the local authority decides to amend the Statement, they must make that amendment within eight weeks of sending the amendment notice to the parents (SEN Reg 17(6). When the Statement is amended a new document must be issued which clearly states that it is an Amended Final Statement and the date on which it was amended as well as the date of the original Statement. Additional advice, such as the minutes of an annual review meeting and accompanying reports that contributed to the decision to amend, should be appended. Parents should be able to clearly see the parts which have been amended (COP 8.131).

As when a Statement is first drawn up, parents will have access to the dispute resolution service set up by the local authority and, importantly, when they receive the amended final Statement, they may appeal to the Tribunal if they are unhappy with Parts 2, 3 or 4.

Parents do not have to wait until the annual review to request a change to Part 4 – the school named in their child's Statement, but there are some time constraints (*see below*).

The local authority does not have to wait until an annual review to amend a Statement. Sometimes amendments may be made in response to a child's changing circumstances. The local authority cannot make blanket changes to all Statements, however, for example if it needs to make budget savings. It must consider each child's needs individually.

The LA decides not to amend the Statement

If the local authority decides not to amend the Statement, following an amendment notice, it must write to the parents explaining why within eight weeks of its letter setting out the proposal. (This does not apply if no amendment notice is issued.)

There is no right of appeal against a refusal to amend a Statement except in relation to Part 4 (school placement) and even this right is limited. If a local authority refuses to name a parent's choice of school, parents have the right of appeal. But local authorities are under no additional duty under 316A to find a mainstream school, even where parents wish this, if the Statement describes special school provision. (*See* Change of school *below.*)

If the local authority decides not to amend Parts 2 and/or 3 of a Statement, despite parents' representations, the remedy is generally for parents to request a statutory reassessment under S328 of the Education Act 1996 (*see page 29*). However, in order to invoke their right to appeal against the content of the Statement they must first cross the hurdle of getting the local authority to agree to the reassessment or going to appeal on this issue too. In the worst cases this could be a drawn-out and stressful process and illustrates the importance of getting the right detail in the Statement when it is first drawn up.

If the local authority refuses to amend a Statement, even though everyone at the review meeting agreed with proposed changes, it may be possible to challenge the LA through the courts or other complaints routes (*see chapter 6*).

Amending the Statement following a reassessment

Local authorities must follow the same procedures as when making a new Statement including issuing a proposed (amended) Statement which will leave Part 4 blank to allow parents the opportunity to state a preference for a school (*see Chapter 4*).

A change of school

Parents may ask for a change in the name of the school on their child's Statement, even if the review did not recommend it. It helps if they give clear reasons backed up by any evidence available.

The local authority must comply with the request so long as it is made more than 12 months after:

- a similar request
- the issue of a final copy of the Statement
- the issue of an amendment to the Statement
- the conclusion of an appeal to the Tribunal over the provision specified in the Statement

(whichever is the latest of these) and subject to the **Schedule 27** conditions set out on page 51.

Following a recent court case (R (on the application of MH) v (1) SENDIST (2) Hounslow London Borough 2004 [ELR 2004 424] it appears that local authorities are under no obligation to apply **S316A** in cases where parents want to move their child from special school to mainstream school by amending the Statement. Their preference could be refused under **Schedule 27**. Although parents have a right to appeal, the Tribunal would also be constrained in the way it looked at the appeal, for example it would not be able to order changes to Part 3 to match mainstream provision. This is an issue likely to be revisited by the courts. Until then, parents would have to ask for reassessment to invoke **S316A** and open the arguments on Parts 2 and 3 of the Statement.

School transfer

When the change of school is from one phase of schooling to another, the Code urges advance planning. So for transfer to secondary school it suggests that the Year 5 review should give clear recommendations as to the type of provision required after primary school. The aim is to give parents of children with Statements the same length of time as other parents to consider appropriate options. The law now requires that the child's Statement be amended by February 15 of the year of transfer in the light of these recommendations. This applies to transfers from first to middle and to higher schools and transfers from primary to secondary. It does not apply for transfers between early years and primary education. It does not apply to transfers between schools at 16 unless the transfer is to a local authority maintained institution which mainly caters for young people aged 16 to 19 (**SEN Reg 19**).

It is good practice for the SENCO of the receiving school to attend the Year 6 annual review for primary pupils whose Statement already names their secondary school. Parents could ask their child's primary school headteacher if this will happen at their child's final review.

Ceasing to maintain a Statement

If there is evidence that the Statement is no longer needed then the local authority can take a decision to cease to maintain it. Such a decision should only be made *"after careful consideration by the LEA of all the circumstances and after close consultation with parents"* **(COP 8:117)**.

This would involve consideration of all the evidence arising from an annual review, including whether the objectives of the Statement have been achieved. The local authority must be satisfied that a child's progress can be maintained from the school's budget and without the need for the extra or different help which the Statement provides and without local authority oversight.

The Code says local authorities could consider the following when making their decision:
- have the objectives been met?
- can the child's future needs be met from school resources?
- can the child access the National Curriculum?
- does the child no longer need daily adult supervision or substantial adaptation of teaching materials to access the curriculum fully?
- can the child cope with everyday social interaction at school?
- has the child significant self-help difficulties that require more provision than is normally available within the school?

(COP 8:119)

If the local authority concludes that the Statement is no longer necessary it must write to the parents informing them of its decision and the reasons and providing copies of any evidence that supports its decision. At the same time parents should be told of their right of appeal to the Tribunal and the time limits for lodging the appeal. They must also be told of disagreement resolution services and that their right of appeal is not affected by any dispute procedure.

The local authority may offer to meet parents to explain its reasons and discuss the provision for their child once the Statement has ceased. The meeting should take place before the Statement and its provisions actually cease but if parents disagree with the decision and lodge an appeal to the Tribunal, the local authority must maintain the Statement until the Tribunal makes a decision or the appeal is withdrawn **(Par 11(5) Sched. 27 EA96)**.

Further or higher education

When a young person moves into further or higher education, and all parties are in agreement about the move, there is no need to continue to maintain the Statement; similarly where a young person moves out of education into employment. But where there is disagreement, for example the parent wants the child to continue at their current school or move to another school, the local authority will need to formally cease the Statement and continue to maintain it until parents have received a Tribunal decision or decided not to appeal.

The local authority was severely criticised by the court in R v Dorset Council ex parte Goddard (1995) where it attempted to arrange matters so that pupils would cease automatically to be registered at a school after their 16th birthday. The local authority cannot make a decision about the child moving into further education until it has checked that a particular further education institution can meet the young person's needs and has offered a place. It should satisfy itself on both counts before taking formal steps to cease to maintain the Statement.

Parents should be aware that if a child moves into further education, for example in a further education or sixth form college, their child's Statement can no longer be maintained. There is no equivalent guarantee of provision geared to the individual's specific needs in the further education sector. The assessment carried out by Connexions when a young person with SEN leaves school (*see page 17*) is not to be confused with the statutory assessment process and will not result in a Statement. Contact SKILL for more information (*details on page 131*).

A young person of compulsory school age placed in a further education college under arrangements allowed at Key Stage 4 (see pages 104-105) will be receiving secondary education, rather than further education, and generally remains on the roll of a school or pupil referral unit so their Statement, arguably, should continue but will need to be amended to reflect the change in provision.

Children placed by the courts

Where a young person with a Statement is detained under a court order or an order of recall by the Secretary of State, the local authority is under no duty to maintain the Statement but the Code recommends that local authorities pass on information to the appropriate institutions including a copy of any Statement and the last annual review report. The local authority should be involved in the young person's exit plan (COP 8.103-4).

Transition review

ACE advice for parents and schools
Use the Transition Review to plan ahead for any special arrangements required for exams.

The process of annual review for students in Year 9 and after is similar to that for younger pupils with a Statement but there is an important difference. The evidence that is collected for the review must have an additional focus on the needs of the young person as s/he moves into further education, training or employment after the age of 16. To this end there must be multi-agency involvement in the Year 9 review. The headteacher must invite social services and should ensure health authorities and trusts are informed. The Connexions service or careers service must be asked to provide written advice and a Connexions personal adviser invited to attend the transition review meeting (SEN Reg 21). It is a condition of the grant of Connexions that they attend this review. If the personal adviser has already been involved with the young person and an action plan has been drawn up, the Transition Plan should build on this. If the young person agrees, the action plan could be circulated with reports prior to the transition meeting.

Parents must be invited to the review meeting and, although under the SEN Regulations the headteacher is not required to invite the student to the annual review, the Code says that the views of young people themselves should be sought and recorded wherever possible in any assessment, reassessment or review from Year 9 onwards (COP 9.55). Where young people can give their views directly, the Code encourages their attendance at the transition review. Some pupils may need to make their views known through an appropriate advocate, however (COP 3.16). There may need to be advocacy and support from the personal adviser, social worker, peer support or others. In reality, parents remain the main advocates for their child at this important time.

The transition review meeting must consider all the same issues as other review meetings, operate to the same timetable and result in a written report to the local authority but the head must also draw up a Transition Plan in consultation with the Connexions Service or careers service.

Connexions

This service for all 13 to 19-year-olds in England gives priority to those young people at greatest risk of not making a successful transition to adulthood. A network of Personal Advisers (PA) provide particular services for young people with special educational needs and those in public care, for example. PAs link in with specialist support services but also sometimes work directly with young people in schools, including those with SEN. Connexions responsibilities stem from legal duties on the Secretary of State under the **Learning and Skills Act 2000.** Connexions is provided mainly by a network of personal advisers – some located in schools – linking in with specialist support services (**COP 10.14 – 10.17**). Under new proposals, Connexions will come under local authority control. Some may change their name but will continue to give careers advice. In Wales, Career Wales provides support at transition review and beyond.

The role of the local authority and other agencies in the transition review and beyond

The Code points out that multi-agency input at Year 9 is important for all young people with SEN. As well as notifying health and social services, local authorities must serve a notice on the Connexions service or careers service for their area. This will list all the children with Statements for whom the authority is responsible who need a transition review.

Local authorities have a statutory duty to consult social services under S5 of the **Disabled Persons (Services, Consultation and Representation) Act 1986**, to establish whether a young person with a Statement is disabled and so may require services from the local authority on leaving school.

Children with significant special needs may be 'children in need' as defined by the **Children Act 1989**. Social services may arrange multi-disciplinary assessments and must establish children's service plans for such children.

The Code says that a social worker should attend the transition review meeting and contribute to the Transition Plan where a young person is in public care or is a child in need. The head should consult the social worker to decide who else should be invited to the review. Birth parents, foster parents and residential social workers may also be involved.

Health professionals already involved in the management and care of the young person should provide advice and, where possible, should attend the transition review meeting. They should advise on services needed and how and when adult services will replace current arrangements.

Transition Plan

After the transition review meeting, the head must draw up a Transition Plan which pulls together information from within and beyond school and describes ongoing school provision under the Statement and post-school arrangements.

Reviews after Year 9

Year 9 reviews are the start of a longer process for making decisions about the young person's future. Reviews after Year 9 will review the Transition Plan and decide whether any additions or amendments should be made. The young person's personal adviser should be invited to subsequent reviews, and should try to attend the Year 11 review in particular. Vocational guidance should include information on Key Stage 4, post-16 options and take into account any aspirations voiced by the young person. Those professionals who know the young person well should be involved. In the young person's final year of school (which may be at the end of year 11 but could be later) the Connexions service has a separate responsibility to ensure an assessment of their needs on leaving school is undertaken and provision identified. The Code says that every effort should be made to link the final annual review meeting and to consider the Transition Plan with the assessment. Where post-16 provision has been identified, heads should invite a representative from that provision to the review. **(COP 9:62)**.

A Pathway Plan building on care and Personal Education Plans, and mapping out education, training and employment will be drawn up with eligible 'looked after' young people by their 16th birthday under the **Children (Leaving Care) Act 2001**.The Pathway Plan is likely to be part of the same document as the Transition Plan and Connexions personal action plan as they fulfil the same function.

Transferring a Statement

When a child with a Statement moves from one local authority to another, the new local authority – if it is in England or Wales – must adopt the Statement of the old authority. The new authority becomes responsible for maintaining the Statement and for providing the special educational provision specified in the Statement. The old authority may also transfer any opinion they have received under the **Disabled Persons (Services, Consultation and Representation) Act 1986** that the child is disabled.

Within six weeks of the date of the transfer the new local authority must write to the parents informing them that the Statement has been transferred and stating whether they propose to make an assessment under **S323 EA96**, or when they propose to review the Statement. They must review it either within 12 months of the Statement being made or previously reviewed or within three months of the date of the transfer – whichever is the latest.

Where the child's move means that they must also move school, the new local authority may arrange for them to attend an appropriate school until it is possible to amend the Statement. If parents were in conflict with their old local authority over education decisions, or if they believe that the provision in the new authority is different, or that their child's special educational needs have changed, or that a fresh assessment by new people would be useful, they should tell the new local authority in writing that they want them to reassess their child under **S328 EA96**.

Parents' action: planning for the annual review

Begin with two sheets of paper. One is to write notes of all the points you want to make in your written advice. The second is to write questions which you can ask at the review meeting.

Your written advice can be just a list of points or you could add evidence for your views such as examples of your child's behaviour at home, letters from other professionals such as a doctor, or details from reviews of your child's Individual Education Plans.

1. Check the aims for your child
Begin with your child's Statement. Find Part 3 which should begin with the objectives – or aims – of the Statement.

Answer the following questions:
- do the aims still seem right for my child?
- is my child making progress towards the aims?

Think about your child. If you think the aims are still right for them, make a note of this.
If you think they should be changed, write down how they might be made better.
If you're not sure how well your child is doing, write down a question for the meeting.
Your child may be close to meeting the aims or they may only be making small steps.
You can check small steps in your child's progress by looking at copies of their Individual Education Plan for the year. These will include short term targets for your child. You could go through the targets with your child and ask them how they feel they have done.

2. Check short-term targets
Now check whether your child has met the targets on the Individual Education Plans. Were the targets too easy or too hard? Are they the right targets focussed on the right area of learning?

Make a note of:
- areas of concern
- improvements noticed by your child and yourself
- any difficulties your child has had
- any action taken by the school
- what worked and didn't work.

3. Check your child's National Curriculum progress
Before the review meeting the school must tell you about your child's progress in the National Curriculum and in any other subjects which your child studies instead of the National Curriculum. They may provide information about your child's progress in basic reading, number and life skills and how they are doing in other areas of the curriculum. This may depend on their age and what level they are working at.

For some children with severe learning difficulties the school may have checked their progress by using the P scales. These measure very small steps of progress. See Supporting the Target Setting Process, DfEE, 2001, for further details about the P scales.

Ask for any information you feel you need to make a proper judgement about your child's progress. You have a right to a copy of your child's school record which includes their school reports and other information such as copies of their IEPs. Write to the head-teacher for this but remember it can take up to three weeks for the school to give it to you and they are allowed to make a reasonable charge.

Any information provided for the review should be translated if necessary to ensure you, and anyone helping you, can take a full part if you have English as an additional language.

Now check how your child is doing. If they have recently been tested or assessed by their teacher, ask how their results compare with others of the same age group. How do they compare with earlier tests they may have taken? Ask the SENCO or headteacher for this information before you write your advice if possible.

4. Check your child's behaviour and attitude

It's important to talk to your child about what they feel about school. What do they like best at school? What is the worst thing about school?

Make a list of help that is working well and the effect on your child.

Make a list of any problems at school affecting your child's behaviour. Can you think of anything that would help?

Has your child's behaviour changed at home or school? Is their behaviour at home different from school? Give examples.

You should now have a list of points about your child's needs and progress. Use this when you check the Statement.

5. Check the Statement

Now look at Part 2 of the Statement and think if it describes your child's needs correctly.

Make a list of any difficulties which you think are missing or not described in the right way. Add this to your written advice.

Now look at Part 3 of the Statement. Does it provide the right kind of help? Is there enough help or is something missing? Make a list of any changes or extra help you think your child needs. Add this to your written advice.

Now ask if your child's progress is so good that your child has met all the aims that the Statement in Part 3. Could your child manage with the sort of help provided by the school to children without Statements? If you think this may be suggested, make sure you know what help this will be. Add any questions to your list to ask at the review meeting.

Chapter six
Appeals and complaints

The aim of this chapter is to explore the avenues available to seek redress when a parent cannot agree with the local authority or has a complaint about how they or their child has been treated. The main emphasis is on the Special Educational Needs and Disability Tribunal (SENDIST) but also covered are disagreement resolution procedures, school and local authority complaints procedures, and complaints to the Ombudsman and to the Secretary of State. Disability discrimination claims are dealt with in the next chapter.

School complaints

Governing bodies are required to set up procedures to deal with all those complaints which currently are not subject to statutory procedures: this includes special educational needs complaints. Under the Education (SEN) (Information) (England) Regulations 1999 (SI 2506) and the Education (SEN) (Information) (Wales) Regulations 1999 (SI 1442), every maintained school is required to publish information about any arrangements made by the governing body relating to the treatment of complaints from parents of pupils with SEN concerning the provision made at the school

If informal discussions do not resolve the issue and the complaints procedures have been exhausted, any of the parties may consider using the statutory SEN disagreement resolution process (*SEN Toolkit para 5 Section 3*).

Schools must have arrangements for parents to appeal to the governing body about curriculum disapplication. (See page 106 for information about appeals and curriculum complaints.)

Resolution of disagreements

Local authorities must arrange to provide for independent people to help prevent or resolve disagreements:
● between authorities (governing bodies and local authorities) and parents about the performance of duties under the Act
● between parents and the school about the special educational provision for their child.
(S332B EA96)

The local authority must publicise the disagreement resolution service (DRS) among parents and headteachers in the area. Schools which may be involved in disagreement resolution include maintained schools and maintained nursery schools, PRUs, city technology colleges, academies and independent schools if they are named in a child's Statement. Disputes between local authorities and academies about admission of children with SEN may be taken to DRS.

In addition, local authorities must inform parents about the procedure when they give notice of a decision not to carry out a statutory assessment, or at the time of a proposed Statement or proposed amended Statement. (*Toolkit para 33 Section 3*). (*See also* SEN Regulations 2001 (England) 2002 (Wales.)

ACE advice for parents
Contact school staff informally in the first place to try sort out any problem about SEN provision. If that fails ask for a copy of school complaints procedures. You could ask the local parent partnership service to help out but remember, they may be there in a neutral role rather than as an advocate for either side.

These procedures do not affect parents' rights to appeal to the Tribunal and parents must be told of this (S332B(6)). However, parents involved in dispute resolution must remember not to let the deadline for lodging an appeal pass. The two procedures can run side by side (COP 2.24). Disagreement resolution should be offered or requested within the two month statutory period for making an appeal to the Tribunal.

More information about the minimum requirement of disagreement resolution services can be found in the Code (COP 2.22). The key principles are independence and neutrality and the child's welfare and needs (*SEN Toolkit, paras 8, 12 Section 3*). The provision of the disagreement resolution service is subject to inspection by Ofsted.

Parents, the school or the local authority can initiate disagreement resolution and the parent partnership service may suggest it. Participation is voluntary and a refusal to participate will not prejudice future procedures e.g. an appeal to the Tribunal. As a general principle, nothing discussed during disagreement resolution should be made available to the Tribunal without the consent of all the relevant parties (*SEN Toolkit, para 25 Section 3*). This could be a minefield for all involved and parents will want to keep a record of what was said or conceded in these meetings.

Parents can be supported by an independent parental supporter. It is not envisaged that the child would be present but his or her views should be heard (*SEN Toolkit, para 45 Section 3*).

Disability discrimination

The Special Educational Needs and Disability Act 2001 (SENDA) extends disability discrimination legislation to education. The Disability Rights Commission has set up an independent conciliation service for disputes arising from the school's duties under the amended Disability Discrimination Act 1995. Agreeing to take part in this process does not prevent the parent from pursuing a claim of discrimination. Most claims will be made through the Special Education Needs and Disability Tribunal (SENDIST). *These are dealt with in Chapter 7*. Claims relating to discrimination in admissions or permanent exclusions will be made through the relevant appeal panels and will follow the normal timetable for such appeals.

The Special Educational Needs and Disability Tribunal

The Special Educational Needs and Disability Tribunal (the Tribunal) is an independent tribunal which hears parents' appeals against certain decisions of the local authority about a child's special educational needs and claims of disability discrimination against schools and local authorities. The Tribunal comes under the scrutiny of the Council of Tribunals whose role is to review the constitution and workings of tribunals. There is a separate tribunal for England and Wales.

Although daunting, most parents perceive the appeal process as fair and are successful in nearly 70% of their appeals (2003/4). Parents should not be over-optimistic because this figure also includes appeals where the Tribunal may have only agreed in part with the parent's case. Sometimes parents may succeed on less significant issues but lose on their main area of concern. Parents are most likely to win appeals concerning the contents of Statements.

The proceedings of the Tribunal are governed by the **Special Educational Needs Tribunal Regulations 2001 (SI600)**. We abbreviate these to **Trib.Regs** in this chapter.

Unlike other education tribunals (for admissions or exclusions for example), the Tribunal is a specialist tribunal presided over by a legally qualified President. Each tribunal that hears a case has a lawyer chairman and two lay members chosen for their expertise in special educational needs. The chairs are appointed by the Lord Chancellor and the lay people by the Secretary of State or The National Assembly for Wales. It acts independently of central government and the local authority. The administration of appeals is handled by a Secretariat.

The Tribunal has a duty, as do schools and local authorities, to have regard to the Code of Practice. In coming to its decision, it will effectively stand in the shoes of the local authority and take the decision again – the point made by the judge in the case of the London Borough of Bromley v SENT (1999) [ELR 1999 260]. He said that in carrying out this duty, the Tribunal also has a supervisory role – to interpret and apply the relevant law. The Tribunal's decision will be taken on the basis of what is appropriate for the child at the date of the hearing (President's direction, 15 March,1995).

The booklet, *How to Appeal*, and video, *Right to be Heard*, produced by the Tribunal, contain useful guidance for parents about the procedures that will be used.

This chapter will look at the law that applies to those procedures and identifies the legal references for the guidance given in the booklet. In addition, it gives practical guidance to parents on how to prepare for the Tribunal and the orders that the Tribunal can make.

Parents may be advised not to draw out negotiations delaying the issue of the final Statement if this delays help to their child especially as they may keep on negotiating in the run up to an appeal hearing. About half of appeals registered are withdrawn before they are heard which in many cases will mean that parents and local authority have resolved their differences. The period waiting for the Tribunal hearing (approximately three to four months) provides an opportunity for the local authority to focus on whether its decision was reasonable, knowing that it will have to be accountable to the Tribunal. Some, if not all, issues in dispute may be resolved before the hearing allowing the Tribunal to focus on any sticking points which are still unresolved. Indeed the Tribunal may adopt any agreed amendments at the hearing. Unfinished negotiations will not usually cause a delay to a hearing.

What issues can't the Tribunal deal with?

The Tribunal cannot deal with an appeal:
- if the local authority refuses a request to change the name of the school to an independent or non-maintained school
- if the local authority refuses to amend the Statement after an annual review

Nor can it deal with an appeal about:
- the way the school is meeting the child's needs
- the way the local authority is arranging for the child to be helped
- the length of time it has taken to assess or statement the child
- the description of the non-educational needs and provision in parts 5 and 6 of the Statement
- Parts 2 and 3 of a Statement (see (4)on the next page) following an amendment a)only to change the name of a school at a parent's request (**para 8 Sched.27 EA96**), or b) after Tribunal orders the local authority to maintain the Statement (**para 11(3)(b) Sched.27 EA96 and S326 (2) EA96**).

What parents can appeal about

A parent can appeal to the Tribunal:

1) If the local authority refuses to carry out a statutory assessment of the child's SEN under s329 or s329A EA96

2) If the local authority refuses to carry out a statutory reassessment under s328 EA96.

In both these cases there is no right of appeal if an assessment has been made in the previous six months.

After hearing an appeal the Tribunal can either dismiss the appeal or order the local authority to arrange for an assessment to be made.

3) If the local authority refuses to issue a Statement after carrying out an assessment under S323 EA96..

After hearing an appeal the Tribunal can dismiss the appeal, or order the local authority to make and maintain a Statement, or remit the case to the local authority for reconsideration in the light of the observations of the Tribunal (S325(3)EA96).

4) If the local authority has made a new Statement, or an existing Statement has been amended*, or the local authority has refused to amend a Statement after reassessment, a parent can appeal against:

- the description of the child's special educational needs in Part 2
- the description of the special educational provision in Part 3
- the school named in Part 4
- the fact that no school has been named in the Statement

(*see* box on previous page and S326 (2) EA96 for exceptions.)

These are appeals under S326(1)EA96.

After hearing the appeal the Tribunal may dismiss it, order the local authority to amend the Statement or order the local authority to cease to maintain the Statement.

The Tribunal will not specify the name of a school unless the parent has expressed a preference for it or it has been proposed in the course of the proceedings by one or both of the parties (S326(4)EA 1996).

The Tribunal need not name a school in Part 4 of a child's Statement if his or her parents have made suitable arrangements (e.g. private education) for the special educational provision specified in the Statement (S324(4A) EA96). Where this applies, Part 4 should specify the type of school which the local authority considers appropriate (S324(4)(a) and COP 8:97). If the Tribunal is satisfied that the parents have made suitable arrangements, the appeal should be dismissed.

There will be circumstances where parents will be unable to apply or appeal for a change of school under para.8 of Sched.27 EA96. This gives a right of appeal only to "the parent of a child for whom a Statement is maintained which specifies the name of a school or institution..." It follows that if no school is named in the Statement, the circumstances for an appeal under that paragraph will not arise. This applies where the parent is making suitable arrangements either by way of home education or education at their own expense.

5) If the local authority refuses to change the school named in the Statement – as long as the Statement or amended Statement is a year old. No similar request can have been made in previous 12 months and the parent can only ask for a local authority maintained school.

This is an appeal under para.8 Sched.27 EA96.

Definition of a child

A 'child' includes:

A person who is not over compulsory school age (S579 EA96)

A person under the age of 19 who is a registered pupil at a school (S312(5) EA96).

If the child has a Statement, the operative time is when the local authority took the decision to cease to maintain. So if s/he was still registered at a school at that point, s/he is a child for whom the local authority has responsibility (S v Essex County Council 2000 [ELR 2000 718]). However, a child who is aged over 16 and not on roll at a school will probably be outside the jurisdiction of the Tribunal.

After hearing the appeal the Tribunal may either dismiss the appeal or order the local authority to name the school or other institution named by the parent. If the parent has made suitable arrangements, and no school is named in the Statement, it follows that there is no right of appeal.

6) If the local authority decides to cease to maintain the child's Statement
This is an appeal under para.11 Sched.27 EA96.

After hearing the appeal the Tribunal may dismiss it, or order the local authority to continue to maintain the Statement either in its existing form or with amendments.

NB If the parents appeal, the local authority must maintain the Statement until the Tribunal makes a decision **(para.11(5) Sched.27 EA96)**.

Who can appeal?

An appeal to SENDIST is a parental appeal. Their appeal will be against the local authority that made the disputed decision. Parents can appeal jointly. If they live at different addresses, the papers will only go to the parent listed first on the appeal form. 'Parent' for the purposes of the Tribunal is a birth parent, any person with parental responsibility or who has care of the child e.g. a foster parent or the authority where the child is subject to a care order (see pages 116-117).

How and when to appeal

The letter from the local authority that informs parents of its decision must inform them of their right of appeal to the Tribunal. The *How to Appeal* booklet issued by the Tribunal contains an appeal form at the back and guidance notes (Tel: 0870 241 2555 for copies). The Tribunal must receive the form no later than the first working day, two months after the local authority notified the parents that they have a right of appeal. If the end of the two months is in August, the parent has until the first working day in September (**Trib.Reg 7(3)**).

The reasons parents give for the appeal must include enough information for the local authority to make its response. If they are not sufficient the President of the Tribunal can direct the parent to give more details and these must be sent within ten working days of receiving the direction (**Trib.Reg 8**).

The President has also said that a late appeal will not be considered to be out of time if the local authority has not included the four points of information on parent's rights listed below in the decision letters it sends them. Each letter must include information about:

1. The parents' right of appeal to SENDIST
2. The two month deadline for the appeal
3. The availability of parent partnership service and of the disagreement resolution services and
4. The fact that the disagreement resolution service does not affect the parents' right of appeal.

Representation

A parent may appoint a representative in the notice of appeal, or at a later stage by notifying the Tribunal in writing. To appoint a representative, the parent must give the name, address and occupation of the person to be appointed (**Trib.Reg 12**). Once a representative has been appointed, the Tribunal will, unless requested otherwise by the parent, send all the documentation to the representative rather than the parent (**Trib.Reg 12(4)**). Parents can conduct the case themselves with assistance from one person if they wish or may appear and be represented by one person, who may be legally qualified. A parent can have more than one representative provided that permission has been given by the President or by the Tribunal hearing the case on the day.

Legal help

Under the legal help scheme administered by the Legal Services Commission, a parent may be able to get free legal help from a solicitor. For the purposes of preparing for the Tribunal this could cover a second opinion, preparing a written case, providing a person to assist at the Tribunal (a Mckenzie friend) but not a representative. For details see www.clsdirect.org.uk

The fact that it is a parental appeal has implications for getting free legal representation if the case goes on appeal to the High Court. Only the parent, not the child, can appeal and as such the means of the parent, not the child, will be taken into account when deciding whether to grant an application for legal representation.

The Tribunal responds

Once it receives the notice of appeal, the Secretary to the Tribunal decides whether the appeal is something it can deal with. If so the parent will be sent a date – the deadline by which the statement of their case and any evidence must be sent in. This is called the case statement period and is 30 working days from the date of notification.

The Tribunal sends a copy of the appeal notice to the local authority which may then put in its written case and evidence within the case statement period.

Before registering the appeal, the Tribunal can give notice to the parent that the appeal is something that cannot be dealt with by the Tribunal and give reasons. The parent can then decide whether the appeal should be entered or not (**Trib.Reg 17(2)**). If there is an obvious error in the notice of appeal the Tribunal can amend it at this point and tell the parent. If the parent is in agreement, the amended appeal notice is entered (**Trib.Reg 17(3)**).

Change of authority

If after the date on which the disputed decision is made, the child moves into the area of a new local authority, the President can order that the name of the new authority is substituted for the name of the old one. The new local authority will then be the party to the appeal and the old one will drop out (**Trib.Reg 43**). All three parties will have the opportunity to be heard about the change.

Parents' Checklist: information for an appeal

As well as a written statement of their case, parents may include other information about their child, for example:
- your child's Statement if s/he has one with your comments
- details of a diary you may have kept on your child's progress. The case statement should contain a chronology of key dates, such as dates of assessments, starting schools, starting therapy, any exclusions from school
- your child's views
- school reports on your child
- your child's Individual Education Plan (these should form part of your child's school record)
- other written evidence e.g. reports from professionals on your child, information from the SENCO or headteacher on strategies and resources available or already in place for your child.

The Tribunal will also need information about the school, for example:
- the school's SEN policy
- the school prospectus
- the school's accessibility plan (see pages 97-98)
- details of the school's facilities, expertise, numbers of children in the school and in your child's class, numbers of children with SEN and with Statements. Some of this information will be in the documents above; you may need to ask for other information from the SENCO or head.

Power to strike out

The Tribunal or the President can give notice to the parent that the appeal should be struck out. The grounds for this are:
- the appeal is no longer within the jurisdiction of the Tribunal
- the notice of appeal, or the appeal is or has become, scandalous, frivolous or vexatious
- the parents have failed to go ahead i.e. want of prosecution.

An appeal can be said to be scandalous, frivolous or vexatious when it seeks to reopen issues that have already been decided upon by a previous tribunal; it then becomes an abuse of process (**Trib.Reg 44**). The broad principle is that at some point the litigation of a particular case should come to an end. However, if there is a change of circumstances or new evidence of sufficient importance, it may be justified to reopen a decided issue (R(A) v London Borough of Lambeth (2001)[ELR 2002 231].

include audio or video tapes but five copies must be enclosed.

New issues, other than those raised in the statement of cases by either party, can be raised at the hearing if it is fair and reasonable but the rules about late evidence should be noted (*see below*).

Preparing for the hearing

At the end of the case statement period, the Tribunal will send a copy of each party's statement of case and written evidence to the other party. This only applies to documents received within the case statement period or within any extension granted by the President (**Trib.Regs 19** and **51**).

The Tribunal will also ask each side about witnesses, representatives, the need for an interpreter and whether the hearing should be in public. Normally the hearings are in private (**Trib.Reg 20**).

If the local authority and parents agree, the Tribunal may decide the case without a hearing, although this is unusual (**Trib.Reg 29**).

In order to enable both parents and the local authority to prepare their cases or to help the Tribunal itself, the President can give directions either on her own initiative or at the request of parents or local authority. The directions may concern disclosure of documents or giving the parents or local authority the right to inspect a document (**Trib.Reg 24**). If a person fails to comply without reasonable excuse to such a direction, they are guilty of an offence (**S336(5) EA96**). The President can also issue a witness summons to require a witness to attend the hearing. (**Trib.Reg 26**). Again if the person fails to attend or produce documents they are guilty of an offence.

Failure to comply with a direction can have serious consequences e.g. if the parent or local authority fails to comply with a direction in the time specified, the Tribunal may dismiss or determine the appeal without a hearing. The Tribunal could go ahead with the hearing, either without telling the party or without the party being entitled to attend or be represented (**Trib.Reg 25**).

Where and when?

Parents and local authority will be consulted about suitable dates for the hearing and this will be confirmed not less than ten working days before the fixed date unless a shorter period has been agreed. The Tribunal tries to hold the hearing as close to parents' homes as possible and usually during normal working hours.

At the opening of the hearing, the Chairman will explain the order in which parents and the local authority will be heard and the order in which the issues will be determined.

Occasionally the Tribunal will adjourn a hearing and may give directions which must be complied with before the hearing is resumed (**Trib.Reg 35**).

Who can attend hearings?

Some people are entitled to be present:
1. the parties – the parents and local authority officers
2. their witnesses – normally a limit of two per side
3. their representatives
4. the child
5. anyone named by a parent to provide support but who will not take part in the hearing: this is normally limited to two people

6. any other parent of the child who is not a party to the appeal
(*see* **Parental Responsibility** *on page 116*)
7. clerk and secretary to Tribunal
8. member of the Council of Tribunals
9. a person undergoing training
10. a trainer of clerks
11. an interpreter or signer

Others can be allowed to attend with the consent of the parties present.

The parent who lodged the appeal may ask a representative to speak for them, but the Tribunal members may still ask them questions, for example about their child's needs at home. Parents do not have to attend the hearing or answer questions but it obviously can make an important difference if they do.

The child can give evidence and address the Tribunal as may a parent who is not a party but apart from that only the persons at 1) to 3) above can take part. If the local authority officer presents the case for the local authority but also gives evidence, s/he is not counted as a witness.

If any party who has been given the proper notice of the hearing fails to attend, the hearing can go ahead and take into account the written representations of the absent party or it can be adjourned (**Trib.Reg** 31).

Late evidence

Late written evidence, if it satisfies certain conditions, can be submitted unless it would not be in the interest of justice. The conditions are that the evidence was not available before the end of the case statement period and a copy had been sent five days previously to the other party and the Tribunal. If it's likely to impede the hearing – because it's very long, for example – then it could be refused.

Otherwise, late written evidence can be submitted at the hearing only if the case is wholly exceptional and there would otherwise be a serious risk of prejudice to the interests of the child (**Trib.Reg33**).

The decision

Normally the decision is given in writing some time after the hearing, although it may be given orally at the end of the hearing. In any event the decision will be written down and sent to the parties. The decision must give "proper, adequate and intelligent reasons" (J v Devon CC, 2001). The Tribunal will also give details of the circumstances when an appeal is possible.

Compliance with Tribunal Orders

The local authority must work within the following timescales if the Tribunal decides it must act:
- to start an assessment or reassessment: four weeks
- to make a Statement: five weeks
- to change a Statement: five weeks
- to change the school: two weeks
- to cancel a Statement: immediately or on the local authority's proposed date.

The Education (Special Educational Needs)(England)(Consolidation) Regs 2001 (SI3455) and the Special Educational Needs Tribunal (Time Limits) (Wales) Regulations 2001 [SI 3982]

Orders for costs and expenses

Orders for costs are very rare and would only be awarded against one party if they had acted, frivolously or vexatiously or wholly unreasonably.

The Tribunal pays travel expenses for parents, their child and whoever comes along to look after the child. These will cover the costs of public transport rather than taxi fares unless you have particular needs. Car parking is not covered. Parents' two main witnesses will also be able to claim travel expenses and can claim a fixed amount for loss of earnings. Parents' representatives cannot claim expenses from the Tribunal.

Remedies after appeal

Both parties can apply to the Tribunal for the decision to be reviewed. The application must be in writing stating the reasons and be made not later than ten working days after the decision was sent.

There are four grounds on which an application for review can be made:
- the decision was wrongly made as a result of an error by Tribunal staff
- a party who failed to appear had good reason not to appear
- there was an obvious error in the decision
- in the interests of justice.

The application can be refused by the President or chair of the Tribunal that heard the appeal. The ground for refusal is that the review has no reasonable grounds of success. There is no obligation to give reasons (C v SENT 1997 [ELR 1997 377]). If the application is not refused at this point, it is heard by a Tribunal that heard the original case or another Tribunal. If the Tribunal is satisfied that any of the grounds are made out it can order that the whole or part of the decision is reviewed and it may give directions to be complied with in advance or at the hearing of the review (**Trib.Reg 37**).

The Tribunal that reviews the decision may set aside or vary it and substitute its own decision, or order a rehearing before the same or a different Tribunal (**Trib.Reg 38**).

Review of a decision of the President

A party or the President may review and set aside or vary any decision of his on three grounds:
1) error of tribunal staff
2) obvious error
3) the interests of justice.

Again application must be made in writing, not later than ten days, giving grounds in full. Parents and the local authority have the right to be heard, unless it is a decision of the President not to extend the parent's time to appeal under **Trib.Reg 7(3)**. In this case the local authority does not have to be heard.

Challenging a Tribunal decision in the courts

There is a right of appeal to the High Court on questions of law but the Tribunal's decision on the facts is final. What this means is that a parent or the local authority cannot appeal simply because they are unhappy with the decision. Either side would have to argue that the Tribunal erred in law by adopting the wrong legal approach, e.g. in the case of Queen on the application (ota) of F v Cumbria CC and Dorsey (Chair SENT) 2001, it was held that the Tribunal erred in law by deciding that the parents' choice of school was inappropriate simply because it included elements of provision that the child did not need. An appeal must be made within 28 calendar days from the date the decision was sent.

If the courts remit a case to the Tribunal to be reheard, parents and the local authority will have an opportunity to submit a supplementary statement of case and further written evidence.

Other routes of complaint

Court action

In recent years judicial review has been the route that the majority of legal actions have been taken by parents or young people against schools, local authorities, appeal panels and Tribunal.
Judicial review is the way that courts supervise how public bodies exercise their powers.
Judicial review covers public bodies including:

- governing bodies of maintained schools and nurseries, academies, CTCs and further education institutions
- local authorities
- appeal panels for exclusions and admissions
- government departments and ministers
- SENDIST
- an independent school (including academies and city technology colleges) in relation to a pupil with a statement of SEN.

The courts do not decide the merits of a particular case in a judicial review, rather they consider how the public body carried out their duties and check that decisions were lawful. Public bodies can be challenged on grounds of:
 1. illegality
 2. unreasonableness
 3. procedural unfairness.

Another potential ground of challenge to a school or local authority is the **Human Rights Act 1998** in which it may be claimed that the public body has acted in a way which is incompatible with one or more of the rights under the European Convention on Human Rights.

Cases must be taken within three months of the date of a decision or failure. Judicial review can result in a public body acting lawfully and in accordance with procedures and/or natural justice. Remedies include:

- quashing a decision and requiring the public body to make the decision again properly. This is the most common remedy
- prohibiting order which prevents the public body acting or continuing to act unlawfully
- mandatory order which requires a public body to perform an action
- injunction – an order which tells a public body to do or not to do something
- declaration which says the decision or act is unlawful. This can include a

declaration of incompatability with the **Human Rights Act**
● damages – an order very rarely made in judicial review but may be awarded, usually in cases where a public body has interfered with human rights.

Negligence

If parents or young people want to recover damages, they will need to show that the local authority or school has infringed their private law rights. The most common type of action is for negligence. Note, however, that although breach of statutory duties might be grounds for judicial review or complaint to the Secretary of State or the Ombudsman, it would not, by itself, lead to a claim for damages.

Negligence is an area of law which is developing very rapidly. The best known case which established educational negligence is the House of Lords' judgment, Pamela Phelps v London Borough of Hillingdon, 2000 [ELR 2000 499]. This determined that a local authority educational psychologist had a duty of care to pupils as well as to her employer, and has opened the door to claims for negligent provision of education. Phelps won damages after arguing that the   psychologist's failure to diagnose her dyslexia reduced her job prospects.

The Phelps action was taken on the basis of a breach of duty of care under common law. Negligence arises when it can be proven on a balance of probabilities that:
● a legal duty of care exists
● the standard of care reasonably expected is breached and
● damage (injury or loss) is suffered as a direct result.

The person who has suffered injury or loss can claim compensation for that. Claims for damages can be made in civil proceedings.

Where an employee is negligent during the course of his or her employment, the employer will be vicariously liable for the negligent actions of staff members including teachers, educational psychologists etc. Educational negligence will still be difficult to prove. Negligence claims can only succeed if the employee acted in a way no other reasonable person of that profession would have done. If their action was in accord with the accepted practice of their profession, even if subsequently it was found to be wrong, negligence may not arise, however. It is not sufficient to show a poor standard of teaching, for example.

In addition, a pupil must show that the negligence caused some measurable harm to the pupil before he can be awarded compensation.

Claims of negligence against each individual professional need to be well founded In a recent appeal case focussing on costs (Clarke v Devon CC 2005 [ELR 2005 375]) the claimant, who had won modest damages following a finding of negligence against one educational psychologist, had part of his costs disallowed because allegations of negligence against other professionals – two headteachers and two other educational psychologists who had had responsibility for the claimant as a child – were rejected by the earlier hearing.

Claims in education negligence are likely to be considered personal injury claims and strict time limits for bringing a claim apply. Expert legal advice should be sought as soon as possible (*see page 131*) and parents are advised to keep copies of all paperwork, including educational records relating to their child's special educational needs.

Complaining to the Secretary of State

If parents think that a local authority or school governors have acted "unreasonably" or that they have failed in their duties under the Education Acts, then they can complain to the Secretary of State or the National Assembly for Wales under **Sections 496** and/or **497** of the **1996 Education Act**. Where there are special procedures for complaint and appeal it is usually necessary to exhaust these before complaining to the Secretary of State or the Assembly. However, a parent could complain if they think that these procedures have not been followed correctly. The Secretary of State has the power to issue directions to the local authority or governing body. However, this power is very rarely used, and an investigation by the Secretary of State can take up to six months or more. Sometimes the very process of making a formal complaint to the Secretary of State acts as a spur to those responsible to try to finally settle the matter.

> The Secretary of State for Education
> Sanctuary Buildings
> Great Smith Street
> London
> SW1P 3BT
>
> Dear Secretary of State,
>
> I am writing to complain and to ask you to use your powers under section 496 and/or 497 of Education Act 1996 because I believe the local authority /school is acting unreasonably / illegally (give details)
>
> Yours faithfully,
>
> Parent

Complaining to the Ombudsman

The Local Government Ombudsman (LGO) investigates complaints of injustice arising from maladministration by local authorities and certain other bodies. The LGO cannot investigate action concerning the teaching, conduct, curriculum, internal organisation, management or discipline in a school. The main test of whether there has been maladministration is whether an authority has acted reasonably within the law, its own policies and generally accepted standards of local administration. The Ombudsman aims to secure satisfactory redress for the complainant and to promote better administration for the authorities. The complaint should be made within a year. The complainant must give the authority the opportunity to investigate and reply to the complaint and the LGO cannot investigate if the complainant has an alternative remedy e.g. a right of appeal to the Special Educational Needs and Disability Tribunal (SENDIST) or a legal action, unless it would not be reasonable to expect the person to go to court or take legal action. Advice and a booklet called *Complaint about the Council?* are available by ringing: 0845 602 1983 or see www.lgo.org.uk

Typical complaints will be about delay in taking action, taking incorrect action, failing to provide information, failing to keep proper records and failure to comply with legal requirements. Examples of the types of injustice that arise from maladministration include missing an opportunity to appeal, a child missing out on education, suffering distress and being put to avoidable time and trouble.

Chapter seven
Disability rights

The legislation

The law on disability discrimination is in the **Disability Discrimination Act 1995 (DDA95)** amended by the **Special Educational Needs and Disability Act 2001** and the **Special Educational Needs and Disability Act 2005**. References in this chapter to the Act refer to the amended **DDA95** unless otherwise stated. Under the Act, schools and local authorities have a duty not to discriminate against disabled pupils. **Part 4** of the **DDA** covers disability discrimination in schools. It applies to existing pupils and those who may be pupils at a school in the future. The **DDA 2005** extends the scope of the **DDA95** by introducing a new duty on public bodies, including schools and local authorities, to promote equality for disabled people.

The Code of Practice for Schools

The *Code of Practice for Schools on the Disability Discrimination Act 1995: Part 4* explains the anti-discrimination duties of schools towards disabled pupils. It can be referred to in legal proceedings. It covers England and Wales. References and abbreviations in this chapter to the Code, are to this code.

Legal duties

Part 4 of the **DDA** requires schools:
- not to treat pupils less favourably for a reason related to their disability without justification (**S28B**)
- to take reasonable steps to avoid putting disabled pupils at a substantial disadvantage (**S28C**)
- to plan to increase access for disabled pupils (**S28D and 28E**).

What is covered?

Every aspect of school life is covered by the duties. Responsible bodies must not discriminate:
- in admissions
- in education and associated services e.g. curriculum, school policies, school trips, school discipline
- by excluding a pupil.

Who is responsible?

The body that has responsibility under the duties is called the responsible body, and this will depend on the function in question i.e. admissions, education and associated services, and exclusions. In maintained schools, the governing body will be responsible for many of the duties, although the local authority will be responsible for the duties in relation to admissions to community and voluntary controlled schools. The local authority will also be responsible for all the functions in pupil referral units and maintained nursery schools. Planning duties apply to governing bodies and local authorities. (*See below.*)

The proprietor – defined as the person or the group of people responsible for the management of the school – is responsible for the duties in an independent school. For example, the governing body is responsible in an academy or city technology college.

Who is disabled?

A disabled child has a physical or mental impairment which hasa:
- substantial
- long-term
- adverse

effect on the person's ability to carry out normal day-to-day activities.

(S1 DDA95)

The issue of who is disabled under the **DDA95** is complicated but it is easier to work through if broken into its constituent parts:
- *physical:* includes sensory impairment
- *mental:* impairment includes learning difficulties
- *substantial:* means 'more than minor or trivial'
- *long-term:* means at least 12 months
- *normal day-to-day activities* include: ability to learn, concentrate, understand and remember things as well as continence, physical co-ordination, mobility and using speech and language.

The legal test of whether an impairment affects normal day-to-day activities is whether the impairment affects one of the categories of 'capacity' listed in **Schedule 1 DDA95**. These are:
- mobility
- manual dexterity
- physical co-ordination
- continence
- ability to lift, carry or otherwise move everyday objects
- speech, hearing or eyesight
- memory or ability to concentrate, learn or understand
- perception of the risk of physical danger.

For the purposes of definition, the effects of medical or other treatments/aids and appliances should be ignored because they tend to alleviate or remove the effects rather than the impairment itself. However, shortsightedness is not normally treated as a disability. Other examples of conditions not normally treated as disabilities are:
- having broken arms or legs (likely to heal within 12 months)
- hay fever (as temporary)
- effects of temporary infections (if less than 12 months duration)
- addiction to or dependency on alcohol, nicotine or drugs
- tendencies to set fires, steal, physical or sexual abuse of others, exhibitionism, voyeurism.

Behaviour difficulties

When does a behaviour difficulty amount to a disability? This is a contentious area and not all pupils receiving help for behaviour difficulties under the SEN framework will have a disability. The Code provides the following guidance:

- a child may have significant behaviour difficulties and these may relate to an underlying physical or mental impairment which amounts to a disability as defined by the Act. If they do, the child will be covered by the Act by reason of the underlying impairment.
- A behaviour difficulty may arise from a mental illness. The 2005 Act removes the requirement for a mental impairment resulting from or consisting of a mental illness to be 'clinically well-recognised'.
- Where a child has a behaviour difficulty for a reason other than a disability, for example arising from social or domestic circumstances, it is likely that such a difficulty is not covered by the legislation. (CODE 4.6)

Other definitions of disability exist. The **Children Act 1989** does not use the same definition of disability as is used in the DDA95. The **Children Act** describes 'children with disabilities' within a wider definition of 'children in need' and therefore eligible for a range of services and support from the local authority (S17 (11) **Children Act**).

There are two forms of discrimination:

1) Less favourable treatment
To establish disability discrimination for this reason, parents will need to ask the following:

- What is the less favourable treatment?
- Is it in one of the areas covered (admissions, education and related services or exclusions)?
- What is the reason for the less favourable treatment?
- Is the reason related to their disability? There has to be a link between the reason and the disability. The law leaves room for an indirect link and the courts have accepted the argument that causal links in disability legislation are much broader than those in other discrimination Acts.
- Is it less favourable treatment than someone gets if that reason does not apply to them? To answer this question, a comparison has to be made between the disabled child with the reason related to their disability, and other children to whom that reason does not apply.

Can the less favourable treatment be justified?
Is the justification material and substantial? The reason for the treatment has to be clearly connected to the circumstances of the particular case and must not be for a reason that is minor or trivial.

Is it the result of a permitted form of selection?
Permitted form of selection, such as entry to a grammar school based on academic ability, would be a legal justification for treating pupils who did not pass an entrance exam less favourably than those who pass. However, the way a responsible body carries out the selection is covered by the duties.

2) Failure to make reasonable adjustments
The second form of discrimination is when a responsible body fails to take reasonable steps without justification and this places the pupil at a substantial disadvantage in comparison with their non-disabled peers.

Case study
The Tribunal struck out the case of a boy with ADHD on the basis that at the time of the alleged discrimination the diagnosis had not been made and therefore his claim was not covered by the **DDA95**. An appeal was lodged to the High Court where SENDIST conceded and the case was remitted to SENDIST for reconsideration. **(DRC/03/8674)**

Case study
A school discriminated against a pupil by failing to give him pastoral support he needed for behaviour problems which arose from his disability. The court agreed that the correct comparator when deciding whether a pupil had been treated less favourably was with a person who was not disabled and who behaved well. It also found that the link between the child's disability and the reason for the less favourable treatment is just that they should be related. It does not have to be specifically caused by the disability. **(McAuley Catholic High School v CC & Ors 2003 [ELR 2004 89]) (DRC/03/8674)**

The case of Buniak v the Jenny Hammond Primary School 2003 is one of the few claims to go to Tribunal which have been widely reported. The Tribunal made some interesting findings although it must be remembered that its decisions do not set a precedent.

The case involved a child with global developmental delay who had been prevented by his primary school from taking part in the school Christmas play, making a card for his mother and going on a school trip. He was also not invited to be in the class photo. The Tribunal found in favour of the child's mother that he had been unlawfully discriminated against. The mother and child received an apology from the school which was ordered to change its policy relating to pupils with a disability and recruitment and retention of staff. All governors and staff were ordered to attend disability equality training.

Interestingly, the Tribunal decided that the school's failure to secure the staffing arrangements set out in the child's Statement was also discrimination. The school had been given the resources to secure appropriate LSA support and had not done so.

The duty on schools to make reasonable adjustments is anticipatory. This means that schools have to think ahead and make changes so that a disabled pupil, or potential pupil, is not at a substantial disadvantage. Remember 'substantial' is 'more than minor or trivial' so it would be relatively easy to put a disabled pupil at a substantial disadvantage.

Reasonable adjustments must be made for disabled children generally but discrimination only occurs if failure to make adjustments leads to the detriment of an individual child.

There are two exceptions to this duty. Schools are not required to:
● provide auxiliary aids or services; these should be provided under the SEN framework
● remove or alter physical features; these are covered by the longer term planning duties. However it may be possible to deal with a physical barrier in a way that falls short of physical alterations but which prevents a pupil being placed at a substantial disadvantage.

The Disability Rights Commission has given the following examples of when failing to make reasonable steps might be discrimination:
● a secondary school failing to make the arrangements necessary for a child to be able to sit public exams
● a deaf pupil who lip-reads put at a substantial disadvantage because teachers continue speaking while facing away from him to write on the board
● a teacher refusing to give her lesson notes to a pupil with dyslexia because "she should take notes during lessons like everyone else".

Deciding what is reasonable involves schools balancing a variety of factors against the potential for a disabled pupil being placed at a substantial disadvantage. For example, schools can take into account:
● the need to maintain academic, musical, sporting and other standards
● the financial resources available
● the cost of taking a particular step
● the practicality of taking a particular step
● the extent to which aids and services will be provided under the SEN framework
● health and safety requirements
● the interests of other pupils and children who may be admitted to the school as pupils.
(CODE 6.30)

Failure to make reasonable adjustments can only be justified if there is a reason which is clearly connected to the circumstances of the particular case and substantial, i.e. more than minor or trivial.

Confidentiality and lack of knowledge

Many changes will need to be made independently of any knowledge of individual pupils and particular disabilities because of the anticipatory nature of the reasonable adjustments duty. But if a school did not know that a pupil was disabled and/or the nature of the disability and if they could not reasonably have been expected to know, this could be a defence to a claim.

It is in a school's interests to be proactive in finding out information e.g. by creating an open and welcoming atmosphere so pupils and parents feel comfortable about disclosure; asking parents during the admissions process about any possible disabilities; providing continuing opportunities to share information (school trip permission; points of transition within the school etc) and by communicating information to whoever may need to know.

Disabled pupils (subject to the school's view of their ability to understand what they are asking to be done and its effect) or their parents may ask for the nature or existence of the disability to be kept confidential. If such a request is made, the nature of the steps to be taken for the pupil may be modified to take account of the request and may limit what the school may be able to do.

Case study
One of the first claims to SENDIST was the case of a six-year-old boy with eczema who was not allowed to wear cotton trousers to school because they were not regulation school uniform (DRC/02/6592). The boy's mother moved him to another school after discussions with the headteacher had borne no fruit. The school claimed that they did not know about his eczema and therefore did not discriminate against him. His mother lodged a disability discrimination claim with SENDIST asking for an apology, a change in school uniform policy and staff training in disability awareness. The claim was settled before the hearing took place.

Case study
A 10-year-old pupil with Chronic Fatigue Syndrome applied to his local grammar school at secondary transfer. He tired easily and found it difficult to concentrate for long periods. His parents approached the school and asked that the two hour examination be split into 20 minute sections. The school refused to make any adjustment on the basis that it would be unfair to other pupils. The parents complained to SENDIST but settled the matter before the hearing on the basis that a reasonable adjustment would be for the exam to be taken in three sections on three separate days. (DRC/02/7239)

Planning duties

Local authorities and schools have planning duties under the DDA95.

Accessibility strategy

LAs must prepare and keep under review an accessibility strategy to:
- increase the extent to which disabled pupils can participate in schools' curriculum (schools for which they are the responsible body)
- improve the physical environment of such schools to increase participation of disabled pupils
- improve the delivery of information to disabled pupils. This must be done within a reasonable time and after taking account of their disabilities and the views of the pupils and their parents.
(28D DDA)

The accessibility strategy comes under the scrutiny of Ofsted. Local authorities need to have regard to allocating adequate resources for implementing the strategy and for any guidance as to the content, form and who to consult on it. (28E DDA). The strategy needs to take into account and inform schools' accessibility plans.

Accessibility plan

Governing bodies of maintained schools and the responsible body for all schools must prepare, keep under review and revise, if necessary, a written accessibility plan. The plan, which is subject to Ofsted inspection, should aim to:

ACE advice for schools
Governing bodies need to think ahead when carrying out their duties. They must keep policies, practices and procedures under continuous review **(Code 6.12 – 6.13).**

● increase the extent to which disabled pupils can participate in the curriculum

● improve the physical environment of the school to increase participation of disabled pupils

● improve delivery of information.

(28D DDA)

The school must have regard to the need to allocate adequate resources for implementing the plan (28E DDA).

Government guidance points out that the plan may dovetail with the School Development Plan and that local authorities and schools share information so that local authority strategies and individual schools' plans inform each other.

An Ofsted report, *SEN and disability: towards inclusive schools*, 2004, has pointed out that many schools still do not have an accessibility plan despite the duty being in place since April 2003. Those that do exist often focus exclusively on the accessibility of buildings. Government guidance *Accessible Schools: Planning to increase access to schools for disabled pupils*, 2002, provides a useful checklist on identifying barriers to access covering the curriculum, built environment and information. Claims cannot be made about accessibility planning. The Secretary of State for Education and Skills, as well as Ofsted, is responsible for ensuring schools carry out these duties.

Disputes

The Disability Rights Commission can take up a case on behalf of a parent or may refer the dispute to the Disability Conciliation Service if the responsible body for the school agrees. This does not stop a parent from taking legal action at the same time or later if they are unhappy with the outcome of conciliation.

Making a disability discrimination claim

Most claims of disability discrimination are heard by the Special Education Needs and Disability Tribunals (SENDIST). These come under the **SENDIST (General Provisions and Disability Claims Procedures) Regulations 2002 [SI 1985]**. However, claims against maintained schools of discrimination in admissions and permanent exclusions are heard by admission appeal panels and exclusion appeal panels and must be made within the timetable for those hearings. Remedies from appeal panels are limited. An independent appeal pane (IAP)l for admissions can only order a school to give a place to a child. It cannot order changes to admission policies, for example. Similarly, the IAP for exclusions is limited to the decisions it may make in law: to uphold an exclusion, reinstate a pupil or decide the exclusion was wrong but that reinstatement is not practical. The Tribunal hears claims of discrimination in admissions and exclusions for independent schools (including academies and CTCs) so parents using these schools are arguably in a better position than those of state school pupils in this respect. Independent appeal panels are subject to judicial review (*see page 89*). Claims against discrimination in fixed period exclusions from maintained schools are heard by the Tribunal.

Claims to Tribunal

Parents need to make the claim to SENDIST within six months of the date when the alleged discrimination took place. If a claim is referred to conciliation, they are given an extra two months from the date of the alleged discrimination.

SENDIST can order a school to use any "reasonable" remedy, except financial compensation. For example, SENDIST might order the school to arrange disability training for staff or to change a policy or procedure. By law a responsible body must carry out a Tribunal decision within a given timescale. If they do not, parents should complain to the Department for Education and Skills or to the National Assembly for Wales. According to SENDIST's annual report 2003/4, the main remedies ordered following successful claims were apologies, training for staff and new school policies. SENDIST cannot order financial compensation.

The Tribunal's decision is final but both sides can ask them to review the decision if they think there are technical problems with the decision and how it was made. Appeals on points of law can be made to the High Court.

SENDIST's booklet How to Make a Claim **is available from the Discrimination Helpline: 0870 606 5750**

Timetable for making a claim

You have 6 months from when the alleged discrimination to make your claim (8 months if you go to conciliation).

To make a claim fill in the form in the middle of the **SENDIST booklet,** How to Make a Claim.

If the Tribunal needs more information they will write and give you 10 working days to send this.

The Tribunal will register your claim and send a copy to the responsible body.

You and the responsible body have 30 working days to make a case statement and provide any more evidence.

During the 'case statement' period, the Tribunal asks you for dates and then informs you when the hearing will be. They write to you at least 10 working days before the hearing to tell you where and when it will be held.

The hearing takes place – it usually takes no more than half a day.

The Tribunal informs you of its decision within 10 working days of the hearing.

You have 10 working days if you want to ask the Tribunal to review its decision and 28 calendar days if you decide to appeal to the High Court.

Parents' action: putting together a claim

One of the stumbling blocks to parents making successful claims is lack of evidence that a child is disabled. The Tribunal's annual report (2003/4) says that more information on how parents could provide this was being made available. Before the Tribunal can consider whether there has been discrimination, it must first decide whether the child is disabled. This is a legal test: it is not enough to say that your child has a Statement or that he is qualified for Disability Living Allowance, you will need to provide evidence.

You should be given the opportunity to bring witnesses to establish whether your child is disabled. The courts have said that this matter cannot be decided at a preliminary hearing without giving the appellants the opportunity to call witnesses (R (Mr and Mrs H) v Chair of SENDIST and R School 2004 [ELR 2005 67]).

Check if your child is a disabled person under the Disability Discrimination Act 1995

Does your child have a physical or mental difficulty?

Is the effect of the difficulty more than minor or trivial?

Are the difficulties likely to last more than 12 months?

If the answer to these questions is yes, try to provide evidence of each point. Describe in detail the physical or mental impairments that affect your child. If you have a formal diagnosis or another report from an expert that explains your child's difficulties, it will be helpful to include this with your case statement. If your child has a Statement, submit this and remember to include the reports (appendices) that accompany it as these may help establish that your child is a disabled person.

The facts of your claim

It is very important that the Tribunal understands in detail why you are making your claim. You should explain each event carefully, giving the dates when things happened. You need to show discrimination in one of the two ways described here:

1. Deciding if the school has treated your child less favourably

What is the reason for treating your child differently?

For example if the school says that your son cannot go on a trip because of his poor behaviour, then the reason is your child's poor behaviour.

Is the reason linked to your child's disability?

If so, consider whether another child for whom that reason does not apply would have been treated in the same way. For example would another child who does not have poor behaviour linked to a disability have been left out of the trip?

If the school can show that they have a strong reason to treat your child less favourably, they may claim justification (see page 95). Be ready to explain your point of view. The final decision on this would rest with the SENDIST or the appeal panel.

2. Deciding if the school has put your child at a substantial disadvantage

This arises if a disabled pupil is at substantial disadvantage compared to other pupils because the school has not made reasonable adjustments which take into account the pupil's needs.

This generally means that unlawful disability discrimination occurs if:

● a disabled child is suffering because they are treated in exactly the same way as non-disabled children and

● the suffering would have been avoided if the school had taken reasonable steps.

Check if your child is at a disadvantage compared with children who are not disabled:

- does your child have to spend more time and effort? or
- is your child inconvenienced? or
- does your child suffer indignity or discomfort? or
- does your child have less opportunity or make less progress?

There could be other reasons that you feel your child is at a disadvantage. Make sure the Tribunal knows about them

Were there reasonable steps that the school could have taken?

You may need to argue that there were steps that the school should have taken to give your child fuller access to life at school. Explain what these steps were but remember that aids and services should be provided through the SEN framework and major alterations to the school come under the planning duty. These fall outside the duty to take reasonable steps. (See page 96)

Any final decision on this lies with SENDIST or the appeal panel. They will have to decide what is 'reasonable' and will take into account a range of factors such as cost, health and safety and academic standards to decide whether the step is reasonable.

Where can I get help with my claim?

ACE's guide, Disability Discrimination, takes you through the steps for putting together your case. Information on how to get a copy at the end of the handbook.

Guides from SENDIST and the Disability Rights Commission also explain how to put in a claim. Advice numbers for these organisations at the end of the handbook.

Chapter eight
A–Z of education issues

Very often special educational needs (SEN) are at the root of other difficulties experienced by children at school. This chapter covers some of the most common such as attendance problems, exclusion and transport difficulties which fall outside the SEN framework.

Admissions

Responsibility for school admissions of children without Statements rests with the governing bodies of voluntary aided and foundation schools, and with the local authority for community and voluntary controlled schools. Children with SEN but no Statement must be admitted in the same way as other children. For children with Statements, the local authority names a school for a child following consultation with governors and after taking account of parental preference. This is dealt with fully in Chapter 4.

Under the amended **Disability Discrimination Act 1995**, admission authorities must ensure that admission arrangements do not discriminate against disabled pupils either on the terms on which the school offers admissions or by refusing or deliberately omitting to accept an application from a disabled person. They must also ensure that the arrangements made for determining the admission of pupils to the school do not substantially disadvantage disabled children. If a parent feels their child has been discriminated against because of their disability they may claim discrimination at an admission appeal.

Admissions arrangements have to be published and, if schools are oversubscribed, pupils should be admitted according to the published oversubscription criteria. Governors should be sure that these criteria are clearly stated and strictly adhered to. There should be agreement as to what constitutes 'special social or medical circumstances'. Details of a school's admission arrangements should be included in the SEN policy and the school prospectus must include arrangements for admission of disabled pupils, steps taken to prevent them being treated less favourably than other pupils, facilities provided to assist their access and details of the school's accessibility plan.

See also the two codes of practice for admissions: *School Admissions*, DfES, 2003 and *School Admission Appeals*, DfES, 2003.

ACE advice for parents
ACE's advice booklet
Disability Discrimination
explains how to make a
claim at an admission
appeal etc.

Attendance

Once a child reaches compulsory school age, parents have a duty to ensure they receive full-time education, which usually means attendance at school. Compulsory school age begins with the term following a child's fifth birthday and ends on the last Friday in June in the academic year in which they turn 16. Failure to secure regular attendance can lead to parents being prosecuted. It is the local authority's duty to enforce school attendance and most employ

ACE advice for parents
ACE's advice booklet
School Attendance
explains where to get
help if your child has a
problem affecting school
attendance and how to
deal with legal action by
the local authority.

education welfare officers to help them do this. Fines may be imposed and Parenting Contracts may be negotiated with parents whose children do not attend as an alternative to prosecution.

Before prosecution, the local authority should first consider applying to the court for an Education Supervision Order under the **Children Act 1989** which allows them to give help, advice and instructions which parents must follow. If the local authority can show that parents are not making an effort to get their child into school, the courts may fine parents up to £2,500 each; impose a Parenting Order which may involve attending guidance sessions; and/or sentence parents to up to three months imprisonment (S444[1A] EA96).

Even if parents can show that they are trying to get their child to school, the courts may fine them up to £1,000 each and impose a Parenting Order if they find that the child is not attending regularly and parents can provide no legal defence (**S444 EA96**). The courts take account of parental income when deciding the level of fines. In some cases they may decide to impose a conditional discharge or an absolute discharge depending on the facts. They will clearly be more sympathetic if parents do their best to get their child to attend.

The defences in law to non-attendance are:

- authorised absence, when the school agrees that your child does not have to be at school
- if a child is ill or there is some other unavoidable reason for their non-attendance
- for religious reasons (e.g. a religious holiday)
- if the school is not within walking distance and the local authority has not provided transport or made boarding arrangements. Walking distance is two miles for children under eight and three miles for those aged eight and above.

Curriculum
Principles of inclusion

The National Curriculum sets out three key principles for inclusion which schools should consider at all levels of curriculum planning:

- setting suitable learning challenges
- responding to pupils' diverse learning needs
- overcoming potential barriers to learning and assessment for individuals and groups of pupils.

The National Curriculum is intended to be accessible to children with special educational needs although some children may have some modification of the curriculum (*see below*).

Key Stage 4

Most maintained schools must follow the National Curriculum but a relaxation of requirements at Key Stage 4 (KS4) enables schools to offer a different curriculum to some young people. This can include extended work experience linked to vocational learning, for example. According to Qualifications and Curriculum Authority (QCA) guidance: "*Disapplication [in KS4] can be considered for any student who would benefit from it. The school is responsible for ensuring that the advantages outweigh any disadvantages and therefore that the disapplication is in the best interests of the student. A decision must be taken for each individual student.*" Science can be disapplied in KS4 to create space for an extended programme of work-related learning.

A programme should:

- offer students experience of working environments and work-related practices
- provide students with the opportunity to develop literacy, numeracy and key skills through such experience
- be designed to complement the education provided through the remainder of the curriculum
- contribute, so far as is practicable, towards approved qualifications, whether vocational or not
- not be possible to provide alongside the full National Curriculum at KS4.

Details of the arrangements for the KS4 curriculum are given in *Changes to the key stage 4 curriculum*, QCA 2003 (effective between 2004/6).

Basic curriculum

The basic curriculum consists of three core subjects: mathematics, English and science, and nine foundation subjects: information and communication technology (ICT), physical education (PE), citizenship, design and technology (D&T), modern foreign language (MFL) (for 11-16-year-olds) history, geography, art and design and music.

Pupils in KS4 must normally study the three core subjects and three foundation subjects (ICT, PE and citizenship). They are also expected to follow one course in each of the following entitlement areas: D&T, MFL, arts, humanities.

Religious education is compulsory in all maintained schools, sex education is compulsory in KS3 and 4 and careers education forms part of the statutory curriculum at KS4. Parents can withdraw their child from religious worship and/or education and sex education if they wish, although human reproduction covered by the science curriculum in KS1 and 2 is compulsory.

At primary level all children in mainstream schools should have access to the national literacy and numeracy strategies alongside the National Curriculum. Differentiation of learning activities may be needed to meet the needs of all children. The *SEN Toolkit* has said that very few pupils should need to be regularly withdrawn from the whole of the literacy hour or daily maths lesson. It accepts that a child may sometimes need some individual tuition or withdrawal from part of a lesson but says schools should aim to include the pupil back in the lesson as soon as possible.

Early years curriculum

The curriculum for early years children is called the foundation stage and the QCA sets out what most children will have achieved in the six areas of learning by the end of reception year. The six areas are:

- personal, social and emotional development
- communication, language and literacy
- mathematical development
- knowledge and understanding of the world
- physical development
- creative development.

In Wales these areas of learning are described as the Desirable Learning Outcomes. (*See also page 25-26.*)

Curriculum exception and modification

Pupils with Statements of SEN may have exceptions or modifications to the National Curriculum written into Part 3 of their Statements (S92 EA02) although it is not necessary for Statements to modify National Curriculum provisions to enable a child to study at a lower level than the majority of pupils of his or her age group. It is particularly important that a broad and balanced curriculum is maintained even where a Statement includes an exception from the National Curriculum. Parents concerned about National Curriculum provisions could appeal to the Tribunal if they disagree with the educational help specified in a new Statement or if they disagree with any amendments made to an existing Statement, including the modification or exception of all or part of the National Curriculum.

Headteachers have power to make temporary exceptions from the National Curriculum for any individual pupil who, for example, has been ill or affected by family distress or difficulty, or who for some reason needs time to adjust following a period out of school. This power to make a general direction to modify or disapply the National Curriculum is given to headteachers by Regulations made under S93 of the Education Act 2002. A headteacher may give a general or special direction to modify or disapply the National Curriculum for an individual pupil on a temporary basis and for a period of no longer than six months in the first instance. Parents have a right to ask the headteacher to give, vary or revoke a direction; if they disagree with the head's decision they have a statutory right of appeal to the governing body. The governing body should hear appeals promptly and allow parents to make representations with a friend or adviser to accompany them if the parents wish. The head and any other specialist staff may also make representations. A governing body can either confirm the head's action or direct them to give, vary or revoke a direction. The head must comply.

General directions may apply to any pupil, including a pupil with a Statement of SEN, at an ordinary or special school who develops temporary problems which it would not be appropriate to reflect in a Statement. With a general direction there is the expectation that at the end of the specified period the pupil will return to the National Curriculum or whatever aspects of it applied to him/her before the general direction came into force. General directions are renewable for up to two further periods of six months.

Special directions have a more limited application and are used by the headteacher to modify or disapply the National Curriculum for up to six months where the headteacher considers that the child has longer-term special educational needs which require the local authority to assess the child with a view to making a Statement. When a special direction expires, one further consecutive special direction can be made. Details of when this would be appropriate are given in guidance on *Disapplication of the National Curriculum* (Circular 0118/2000 for Key Stages 1 and 2).

Curriculum complaints

Parents complaining about any aspect of the curriculum (e.g. the National Curriculum, religious education, collective worship, external qualifications or syllabuses, provision of information, charging for school activities, or appeals regarding disapplication directions) should direct their complaint initially to the headteacher or the governing body. Local authorities have separate procedures for handling complaints about the actions of governing bodies in relation to the curriculum and if parents are not satisfied with the response of the governing body to their complaint, they should take the matter up with the local authority under S409 EA96 (as amended). This applies to curriculum complaints about any maintained school.

Target setting for children with SEN

Target setting is an established process in schools but children with SEN are sometimes ignored in the drive for school improvement. Useful guidance gives a lead on how even children with significant SEN can be the focus of raising standards. *Supporting the target setting process* (revised March 2001) describes how P Scales can help schools measure small steps in achievement. They provide descriptions of attainment below level 1 and within levels 1 and 2 for English and mathematics. A scale for personal and social development is also included and governing bodies may consider additional targets focussing on areas such as behaviour.

In Wales the curriculum authority, ACCAC, has issued guidance which takes a similar approach. *A focus on achievement – guidance on including pupils with additional needs in whole school target setting,* 2002, describes different ways of measuring small steps of achievement. *"Adopting a range of methods and approaches is likely to be in the best interests of schools, while teachers are often empowered by developing or adapting published schemes to ensure that materials are appropriate to their school context and stage of development,"* says the guidance.

National tests and assessments

National tests, often called SATS, are designed to be taken by the majority of children in maintained schools at the end of each key stage.

The QCA in England and ACCAC in Wales allow for special arrangements to be made to enable children with SEN to participate. Braille and modified test papers for visually impaired children are available, for example. These are set out in detail in *Assessment and Reporting Arrangements* published by QCA for each key stage and *Statutory Assessment and Reporting Arrangements* published by ACCAC for each key stage.

Special arrangements should be focused on the assessment needs of the individual pupil and may be appropriate for pupils with a Statement or undergoing statutory assessment; those receiving help at School Action or School Action Plus; and pupils whose disability or emotional, social or behavioural difficulties make them unable to sit and work at a test for a sustained period.

The QCA says that special consideration cannot be applied retrospectively so schools need to consider what arrangements are needed before the tests take place.

With a few exceptions, all children in their final year of Key Stages 1, 2 and 3 must be assessed. This includes children in special schools and those attending pupil referral units on a part-time basis who are still on a school's roll. Children who may be older or younger than most of the children taking tests because they are not being taught with their chronological year group, will be assessed at the point where they are moving on to the next key stage programme of study. They should not be assessed more than once at the end of any key stage. In Wales there are proposals to make Key Stage 2 tests optional but teacher assessment in the core subjects will remain statutory.

Some children will only undergo teacher assessment and will not be entered for the national tests. Schools must report the child's assessment levels to parents. For children who have special educational needs, the QCA says they should always provide more detailed information on the child's progress in relation to the curriculum which s/he is following.

The QCA gives examples of which children need not take the tests:

- a child recently arrived from a different educational system where the school has not enough time to reach a judgement about whether the child could access the tests
- a child with a disability who cannot access the tests even with special arrangements
- a child who has had spells in hospital or has been home educated or excluded and needs time to adjust to school life
- a child who is experiencing severe emotional problems
- a child who has physical or severe learning difficulties and is working at lower levels of the National Curriculum for their age e.g.
  - children in their final year of Key Stage 3 who have been assessed as working at level 3 or below in English or level 2 or below in maths and science
  - children in their final year of Key Stage 2 who have been assessed as working at levels 1 or 2 of the National Curriculum
  - children in the final year of Key Stage 1 working at level 1 will not take tests in English and maths, but will undertake tasks in reading and writing and maths; spelling tests are optional for children working at level 1 in writing.

The headteacher makes a final decision about whether a child takes a test but should discuss the child's circumstances with his or her parents and teachers; consult with educational psychologists, medical officers or other specialist staff; and consult with the local authority (usually the assessment co-ordinator). A decision not to allow the child to take the test is made under **Ss92 or 93** of the **Education Act 2002**. It should be reported to the child's parents in writing and should include information about their right of appeal to the governing body. Copies should go to the chair of the governing body and the local authority assessment co-ordinator. A copy should also be placed on the pupil's educational record.

Parents' requests and appeals

Parents may ask the head not to enter their child for national tests. The QCA says that it would not be appropriate to not enter a child or to modify the tests *"simply because the parents report that the pupil would find them stressful or because of opposition to the assessment"*.

Heads must respond to a formal request from a parent within a fortnight giving reasons. If the head refuses, the parent has the right of appeal to the governing body. Parents also have the right to appeal under the same provisions of the **Education Act 2002** (*see above*) if they disagree with a proposal not to allow their child to sit the tests. The governing body is expected to hear the appeal "with all due speed" and allow representations from parents, headteacher and any specialist staff. Parents should be allowed to be accompanied by a friend if they wish. The governing body may either confirm the head's action or direct him or her to take any other action they consider appropriate. If parents are dissatisfied they may make a complaint to the local authority under their **S409** curriculum complaint arrangements (*see above*).

Examinations

Pupils at the end of Key Stage 4 are normally assessed by public examinations. The Joint Council for Qualifications (www.jcq.org.uk) sets out regulations and guidance agreed jointly by the awarding bodies for the main qualifications taken by pupils. The awarding bodies agree special arrangements or consideration for certain pupils.

Candidates with a Statement do not automatically qualify for special arrangements but the annual review held before the candidate begins coursework should consider the young person's possible needs at exam time. The Joint Council's guidance lists the type of help which may be appropriate in relation to the four areas of need identified by the SEN Code:

- Communication and interaction – may have problems with written communication: they may need to use word processors, be given more time or have a scribe.
- Cognition and learning – candidates with learning difficulties, for example, may be eligible for extra time or reading/writing assistance.
- Sensory and physical needs – candidates with these disabilities may require modified papers and a practical assistant.
- Behavioural, emotional and social needs – these candidates may require supervised rest periods, separate invigilation or alternative accommodation arrangements. In some cases extra time, readers and/or scribes may be allowed.

Awarding bodies will make decisions about special arrangements according to the circumstances and needs of the individual candidate. For certain groups they will require evidence of need and a history of provision during the course. The evidence in the case of learning difficulties must be either a Statement of SEN relating to the candidate's secondary education or a report from an educational psychologist or appropriately qualified teacher made after Year 6/Key Stage 2. Heads of exam centres (usually the headteacher) will apply for special arrangements. Some arrangements may be decided by the head of centre – for example the granting of additional time up to a maximum of 25% of exam time, and/or rest breaks, to exam candidates.

Special consideration may be made if a candidate is affected by circumstances beyond his or her control e.g. recent personal illness, accident, bereavement or if the special arrangements made in respect of their permanent or long-term disability proved inappropriate or inadequate.

Fuller details of the regulations and guidance relating to candidates with particular requirements are available from the Joint Council (www.jcq.org.uk). *See Access Arrangements and Special Consideration Regulations and Guidance,* 2004.

Section 15 of the **Disability Discrimination Act 2005** makes it unlawful for general qualifications bodies to discriminate against disabled people in relation to the award of prescribed qualifications. It inserts **Chapter 2A (Ss31AA to 31AF)** into **Part 4** of the **DDA**. These provisions prohibit unlawful discrimination against disabled people by general qualifications bodies in relation to the award of relevant qualifications. A "relevant qualification" will be prescribed in Regulations and will include A-levels, GCSEs and other non-vocational qualifications. **Section 31AB and 31AC** define what is meant by unlawful discrimination in this context and what is meant by unlawful harrassment. The definitions mirror those which already apply to qualifications bodies which confer vocational qualifications under **Ss14A and 14B (Part 2 DDA95)**.

Definitions
Special arrangements are approved before an examination or assessment; special consideration is given following an examination or assessment to compensate a candidate who has a temporary illness, injury or indisposition at the time.

A general qualifications body can only justify less favourable treatment in applying a competence standard if they apply the standard equally to everyone and if this is a proportionate means of achieving a legitimate aim e.g. demonstrating that a person has a particular level of competence or ability.

A body subjects a disabled person to harassment where, for a reason which relates to their disability, the body engages in unwanted conduct which has the purpose or effect of:

a) violating the disabled person's dignity, or

b) creating an intimidating, hostile, degrading, humiliating or offensive environment for him or her.

S31AA

In certain circumstances general qualifications bodies must make reasonable adjustments where disabled people suffer substantial disadvantage in comparison with others (S31AD). There is no duty to make reasonable adjustments in relation to competence standards, but the duty is imposed where bodies apply provisions, criteria or practices to disabled people e.g. the arrangements made for disabled people when they sit exams.

Exclusions

ACE advice for schools
Make sure your discipline policy has been reviewed to take account of disability discrimination. Remember, schools should take reasonable steps to ensure that disabled pupils are not substantially disadvantaged or treated less favourably, for example, disciplined for behaviour that is linked to a disability. Equal treatment may amount to discrimination.

Government guidance states that while a pupil is being assessed for special educational needs headteachers should make every effort to avoid exclusion. It also points out that statemented pupils should be excluded only in the most exceptional circumstances and that schools should "make every effort to avoid excluding pupils who are being supported at School Action or School Action Plus".

The **Disability Discrimination** Act **1995** (as amended) states that it is unlawful for a school to discriminate against a disabled pupil by excluding him or her whether permanently or temporarily (28A). *(See Chapter 7)*

Despite the law and guidance, almost two thirds of children permanently excluded from English schools in 2003/4 were officially recorded as having special educational needs. The reasons are complex but the reality is that many of these children must go through the trauma of exclusion before their needs are met. Many more lose out on their education when a suitable alternative school is not found. A large proportion of the children educated in pupil referral units have special educational needs.

Parents whose children are excluded can receive a free advice pack on putting together their case for appeal from the Advisory Centre for Education (ACE). Around three quarters of the callers on our exclusion advice lines have children with special educational needs. Phone the information line (0207 704 9822) for a pack and details of our freephone helpline.

Schools should always monitor the number and reasons for exclusions and question whether better pastoral care or earlier intervention could prevent some of them from arising. Pupils who have emotional or behavioural difficulties should be referred for support long before exclusion becomes the inevitable outcome. Normally a pupil who is facing permanent exclusion should have been supported by either a Pastoral Support Programme or an Individual Education Plan which can include pastoral support. The local authority arrangements for behaviour support should describe help available for staff (such as behaviour management training) and for pupils (such as or counselling services or places in specialist units).

Only the headteacher can exclude a pupil from school (or if absent the next most senior teacher) but s/he must act within any broad statements of policy on behaviour and discipline in the school that the governing body has agreed. Parents of excluded pupils can state their case to the governors (usually a discipline committee consisting of three or five governors), who must decide whether or not to uphold an exclusion. For permanent exclusions, parents can also appeal to an independent appeal panel if the governors uphold the exclusion. Claims of disability discrimination relating to permanent exclusions from maintained schools are made to this panel. Claims about fixed period exclusions and all exclusions from independent schools (including academies) are made to the Special Educational Needs and Disability Tribunal.

Permanently excluded pupils with Statements should receive full-time provision like any other excluded pupils (unless the Statement provides for fewer hours for a particular reason). Local authorities are expected to make this provision from the 15th school day following the exclusion. The DfES guidance says that *"if a statemented pupil is unable to meet the full-time requirement for their key stage, but can do so in the longer term, their Statement should be amended to set out the milestones in a staged return to full-time hours"*.

Exclusions at lunch time are regarded as fixed period exclusions. In England each lunch time exclusion counts for half a day; in Wales it counts for a quarter of a day. Guidance from the DfES and from the National Assembly say that lunch time exclusions should be a short-term measure only.

Very often parents of children with SEN tell ACE that they are asked to keep their child at home over lunch time. While parents have the right to take their child home for lunch, they should not do this under pressure. 'Voluntary' exclusions mean that parents lose their right to make representations to the governors.

Improving Behaviour and Attendance: Guidance on Exclusion from Schools and Pupil Referral Units, 2004, and *Circular 10/99 Secretary of State's Guidance on pupil behaviour and attendance* (revised June 2004).

Welsh Assembly guidance *Pupil Support and Social Inclusion*, Circular 3/99 (Chapter 6 and Annex E of Circular 3/99 is replaced by *Exclusion from Schools and Pupil Referral Units* (Circular 1/2004 amended by Circular 1(A) 2004).

Further education

The law regarding the provision and funding of post-16 education for students who have special educational needs is complex and parents who may have struggled for the needs of their child to be met in school often face reopening the arguments once they reach 16. Many will want their child to remain in school where they can retain the safeguard of a Statement. For the purposes of the law, a young person remains a child if he is a registered pupil at a school and is under 19 (S312 (5) EA96).

Although the Learning and Skills Council (LSC) is responsible for funding post-16 special educational needs in schools, this has not in any way altered local authorities' statutory duties and responsibilities under the **Education Act 1996** to young people aged 16-19 with SEN who are registered at a school. Local authorities continue to receive and distribute all the funding and retain their responsibilities for the assessing, statementing and review processes, including arranging special educational provision. The only difference is that

ACE advice for parents
If you want your statemented child to continue to stay at school post 16, make sure the local authority knows this. If it disagrees and suggests your child attends a FE college, it should then go through the process of ceasing to maintain the Statement. If the local authority believes you agree with the move, it need not go through this process.

post-16 funding for all pupils now comes to the local authority via the LSC. The LSC, as a condition of its funding, requires local authorities to maintain Statements until the end of the academic year in which the young person becomes 19 (COP 9.61).

If a young person with a Statement leaves school, the local authority is no longer responsible for their education. Many young people with special educational needs move into further education colleges – free-standing institutions that receive their funding from the LSC. The Council must have regard to the needs of people with learning difficulties and has a statutory duty to take account of assessments that are arranged by Connexions. Under S140 of the **Learning and Skills Act 2000,** Connexions must undertake an assessment of a young person's final year of school and identify provision. This should be linked to the final annual review of the Statement. The Code recommends that the LSC at the local level and Connexions work closely with schools and local authorities to ensure that appropriate support and funding arrangements are in place for provision set out in young people's Transition Plans. Young people without a Statement but with SEN who might have difficulty transferring to further education or training after Year 11 should also have a needs and provision assessment – this is a condition of the government grant given to Connexions (COP 9.67).

LSC guidance to colleges on providing additional learning support (ALS) recognises that useful information will be contained in pupils' Statements and recommends that colleges and other providers have regard to this.
The guidance suggests the following types of ALS as appropriate:

- additional teaching – either to reduce class sizes or to provide support in or out of the class.
- other specialist staffing – for example, personal care assistant; mobility assistant; reader; note-taker; amanuensis; in-class support assistant; dedicated technician (for supply, maintenance and training in the use of equipment for learners with disabilities and/or learning difficulties); specialist tutor (for example, teacher of the deaf, or teacher of learners with dyslexia); communication support worker (for example, Braillist or support for deaf learners); additional tutor support for counselling and guidance for individual learners that relates to his or her disability; material adaptation worker; or educational psychologist.
- funding for a speech therapist and/or a physiotherapist (LSC guidance says that such support should be funded by the college or provider and is eligible for ALS funding but adds the following rider: *"Normally, the provision of such support should follow an assessment by an appropriately qualified person. Where speech therapy or physiotherapy is not identified in a learning agreement as necessary to enable a learner to achieve his or her learning aims and does not meet the definition of ALS, funding should be sought from the relevant health authority".*
- assessment and review pre-entry and on entry, on-programme and on exit, where this involves specialist inputs or a higher level of input than that provided on the individual's learning programme.
- personal counselling – where such support is necessary to enable a learner to achieve his or her learning goal.
- transport between sites and to other off-site activities for learners with mobility difficulties, but not home-to-provider transport.
- administration linked directly to individual learners that is in excess

of usual requirements – for example, time spent negotiating or delivering special examination facilities.

Some young people, who generally cannot have their needs met in a local further education college, may attend specialist 'out of sector' colleges. Decisions about whether a young person will be placed in such a college are made in accordance with criteria set out by the LSC.

The **Special Educational Needs and Disability Act 2001** made it unlawful for bodies responsible for a further education institute to discriminate against a disabled person in respect of admissions, exclusions or student services without lawful justification.

Further information from SKILL (the National Bureau for Students with Disabilities (address on page 131)

Independent schools

Local authorities can use independent and non-maintained schools (S18 EA96). If they name an independent school in a child's Statement, they must normally pay the fees for the education provided. However, if the parents choose to place a child with a Statement in an independent school at their own expense, the local authority must be satisfied that the school can make special education provision that meets the child's needs and there is a realistic possibility of parents funding the placement for a reasonable period. Once satisfied they are not required to specify the name of the school in Part 4 of the Statement but they must state the type of provision. In some cases local authorities will fund the help which is additional to or different from that received by other children but not the normal fees for a place at the school.

If the local authority is not satisfied that suitable arrangements have been made, they will name a different school which they feel appropriate.

Local authorities may only name an independent school in a Statement which is approved by the Secretary of State (or the Secretary of State may consent to a particular child being educated there). **The Education (SEN) (Approval of Independent Schools) Regulations 1994 [SI 651]** prescribe the requirements on independent schools seeking approval.

City colleges (including academies and CTCS)

Academies, city technology colleges and city colleges for the technology of the arts (collectively described as city colleges) are independent schools funded by the Secretary of State under S482 of the Education Act 1996. Although officially deemed independent schools, and therefore not subject to education legislation, funding agreements with the DfES set out the duties of academies and city colleges. The Regulations about Secretary of State approval described in the previous paragraph do not apply to them. (**Education (Special Educational Needs) (Approval of Independent Schools) (Amendment) (England) Regulations 2002 [SI 2072]**).

Annex 3 of the model funding agreement between the Secretary of State and academies includes the following points:

1. Academies must have regard to the SEN Code and any guidance about admission of pupils with SEN into mainstream schools.

2. The governors of academies must designate a person responsible for certain duties with regard to SEN. These duties correspond with those set out in **S317** of the **Education Act 1996**.

Information rights

A Statement forms part of a child's educational record and parents have a right to a copy. A Statement must not be shown to any unauthorised person without the consent of the child, or his or her parent's consent where the child is too young or has insufficient understanding to give informed consent. Statements must be stored so that unauthorised people do not have access to them. (*See* **Keeping a Statement,** *page 63*.)

The **Data Protection Act 1998 (DPA)** gives anyone who is the subject of personal data a general right of access to the data which relates to them. This includes children and young people and parents acting on their behalf.

Both manual and computerised personal information, including that held by schools, is subject to the Act. The Act also sets out specific rights for pupils in relation to educational records held within the state system.

Along with the rights of pupils under the DPA are those of parents under the **Education (Pupil Information) (England) Regulations 2005 [SI 1437]** and the **Education (Pupil Information) (Wales) Regulations 2001 [SI 1026 W123]**. In effect this means that both parents and pupils are entitled to a copy of the school record for the child although, in the case of pupils, schools need not comply if it is obvious that the child does not understand what they are asking for.

Requests to see or receive copies of records should be made in writing to the governing body which must respond within 15 school days under the Regulations. Personal data requested under the DPA must also be provided within 15 days when this is requested by the subject of the record (the pupil or his or her parent in relation to school records) but for other types of record it is up to 40 days.

Under the DPA, pupils are also entitled to be given a description of the personal data which makes up the record, together with details of the purposes for keeping the information and, where known, the sources of the information, and the individuals or organisations to whom the data may have been disclosed.

Schools should not disclose anything on pupils' records which would be likely to cause serious harm to the physical or mental health of the pupil or of anyone else, including anything that suggests that they are, or have been, either the subject of or at risk of child abuse.

If a pupil's request for information under the Act is refused or ignored, the matter can be referred to the Information Commissioner or an application for disclosure can be made to a court. Parents can pursue a case on behalf of their child.

Parents having difficulty accessing records under the pupil information regulations may complain to the governing body, then the DfES or, as a last resort, the courts.

Under the information Regulations, mentioned above, schools must transfer school records when children move to a new school within 15 school days of the child ceasing to be registered at the old school. Secondary schools should receive the school records of all pupils identified by their primary schools as having special educational needs. This will include any detailed background information collated by the SENCO; copies of IEPs and any Statements of special educational needs. The Code points out that when schools transfer records to other schools, the full pupil record will include all the information held by the SENCO including IEPs. It follows that this same information must also be made available to pupils and parents on request (COP **5.24, 6.26**).

When local authorities issue a proposed Statement to parents they must also provide copies of the advice reports prepared as part of the statutory assessment. The advice must also be provided to parents following a statutory reassessment even if the local authority decides not to make an amendment. Copies of advice reports provided as part of the annual review must also be provided for parents.

While the Regulations do not cover the need to provide copies of advice reports to parents following a statutory assessment when a local authority decides not to issue a Statement, these reports would generally be accessible under the **DPA**.

School policies and other information such as governing body minutes, except for confidential items, are available on request **(School Governance (Procedures) (England) Regulations 2003 [SI 1377] and Education (School Government) (Wales) Regulations 1999 [SI 2242]).** The **Freedom of Information Act 2000** which came into force on January 1 2005 also gives the public a general right of access to information held by and about public authorities; these include schools and local authorities. Schools are under a duty to provide advice and assistance to anyone requesting information. Enquirers do not have to say why they want the information and they are entitled to be told whether the school holds the information (this is known as the duty to confirm or deny) and, if so, to have access to it. Access can include providing extracts of a document or a summary of the information sought, or access to the original document. However, the Act recognises the need to preserve confidentiality of sensitive information in some circumstances and sets out a number of exemptions. As with request for school records, requests for information should be in writing, which includes fax or email.

Any complaints about information, such as a failure to provide documents requested or disagreements with information in a pupil's education record, should be made through the school or local authority complaints procedure.

If this does not resolve the issue, the Information Commissioner enforces and oversees the **Data Protection Act 1998** and the **Freedom of Information Act 2000.** Complaints should be addressed to the Information Commissioner, Wycliffe House, Water Lane, Wilmslow, Cheshire SK9 5AF.

Language differences

Children must not be regarded as having a learning difficulty solely because the language or form of language of their home is different from the language in which they will be taught. At the same time, when children who have English as an additional language make slow progress, it may be that they have learning difficulties.

Schools are advised at an early stage to make a full assessment of the exposure such children have had in the past to each of the languages they speak, the use they make of them currently and their proficiency in them. The Code points out that this information about language skills will form the basis of planning help for any learning difficulties and in planning any additional language support that is needed. Where there is uncertainty about an individual child, schools should make full use of any local sources of advice relevant to the ethnic group concerned, drawing on community liaison arrangements wherever they exist.

Children with a learning difficulty or developmental delay, and whose parents do not have English as a first language, are among those likely to be particularly disadvantaged if any SEN are not identified quickly.

Translators and interpreters

Local authorities are advised to provide parents and relevant professionals with access to interpreters and translated information material to aid early identification of learning difficulties. Similarly local authorities conducting assessment and statementing or maintaining a Statement should seek advice from bilingual support staff, teachers of English as an additional language, interpreters and translators and other local sources of help as appropriate, to ensure that parents and children are involved in all aspects of the process. The timescale for planning the annual review should take account of time needed for translations, availability of interpreters, help required by professionals from the child's community to contribute to the review process, and attendance of a bilingual support teacher or teacher of English as an additional language to support the child and family.

Parental responsibility

This handbook explains the part that parents play in the process of getting extra help for their child. But who exactly are parents? Is it only the birth parents of a child who are entitled to take part in the assessment and statementing procedures? What about other relations, step parents and foster parents – do they have a part to play? According to the legislation they do, and the definition of a parent includes not only those who have parental responsibility for a child but also those who have care of a child.

The model for parenthood in the **Children Act 1989** recognises that being a parent is a matter of having responsibility for a child rather than having rights over him or her. Parental responsibility is defined as *"all the rights, duties, powers, responsibilities and authority which by law a parent of a child has in relation to the child and his property"* **(S3(1) CA89)**.

S576 of the **Education Act 1996** defines parents as including birth parents plus any person who, although not a birth parent, has parental responsibility under the **Children Act 1989**, and any person who, although not a birth parent, has care of a child or young person.

Parental responsibility under the **Children Act 1989** can be acquired through being granted a residence order, being appointed a guardian, being named in an emergency protection order or adopting a child. Unmarried fathers may acquire parental responsibility either by registering the birth with the child's mother, by formal agreement with the mother, or by court order.

It is clear then that more than one person may have parental responsibility for the child at the same time. Court orders under **S8** of the **Children Act 1989** settle areas of dispute about a child's care or upbringing and can limit an individual's parental responsibility.

If a child is 'looked after' by a local authority, they may either be on a care order or be voluntarily accommodated. A care order places a child in the care of a local authority and gives the authority parental responsibility for the child. The local authority can determine the extent to which this responsibility will be shared with the parents. A child might be looked after by the local authority in a residential or foster placement, or might live at home.

A child may also be accommodated by the local authority under voluntary arrangements with the child's parents. In these circumstances the parents will retain parental responsibility acting so far as possible as partners with the local authority. Where a child is looked after by a local authority day-to-day responsibility may be with foster parents, residential care workers or guardians. In either case the headteacher, in consultation with social services, should decide the extent of the contribution to be made by the child's parents, the residential care worker or foster parents and the social worker at the child's annual review. The DfES guidance, *Who does what*, 2004, has detailed guidance on when carers and social workers should be involved in the education of children in care.

Under education law 'having care of a child or young person' means that a person who the child lives with and who looks after the child is considered to be a parent in education law. It follows then that foster parents who have care of a child can pursue a case to Tribunal on behalf of their foster child. This was confirmed by the courts in the case of Fairpo v Humberside County Council 1996 [ELR 1997 12], where it was judged that where a local authority which had parental responsibility disagreed with the foster parent about the child's education, the foster parent should be able to test the issue before the Tribunal.

Service children

The Children's Education Advisory Service (CEAS) oversees the education of the children of UK service personnel living abroad. It provides schooling for those children and also includes an advisory service which offers assistance and advice to service personnel who are parents of children with special educational needs.

CEAS makes provision for some children with SEN both in mainstream classrooms and special units. For children of service families living abroad, the service, rather than a local authority, will identify and where necessary assess and draw up a Statement for children with special educational needs at CEAS schools and pre-schools. Parents of children with SEN are advised to register with the UK office to discuss provision. (HQ Children's Education Advisory Service (UK), Trenchard Lines, Upavon, Pewsey, Wiltshire SN9 6BE (Tel: 01980 618244).

Service families in the UK will use the appropriate local authority in the same way as other families. If the local authority is undertaking a statutory assessment, it must seek written advice from the service where the child's parent is a serving member of the armed forces.

Sex and race discrimination

The **Sex Discrimination** Act **1975** prohibits discrimination on the basis of marital status or gender and applies to both men and women and boys and girls. Local authorities and schools should ensure no discrimination on gender grounds although admission arrangements for single sex schools are exempt.

The **Race Relations Act 1976** makes it unlawful for schools and local authorities to discriminate on race grounds in the provision of any of their services. This includes discrimination in admission of pupils, the treatment they receive as pupils and in their exclusion from school.

The **Race Relations Amendment Act 2000** imposes a legal duty on schools and local authorities to promote good race relations and equality of opportunity. ACE publishes a *Short Guide to the Law on Equal Opportunities and Human Rights Legislation* covering sex, race, and disability discrimination legislation in schools, and the **Human Rights Act 1998**.

Sick children

Disability discrimination legislation has had a major impact on the way schools and authorities are expected to care for children with medical needs. Schools and nurseries should be making reasonable adjustments for disabled children including those with medical needs.

DfES statutory guidance, *Access to Education for Children and Young People with Medical Needs*, 2001, covers the responsibilities of schools, local authorities and hospital teaching services for pupils with medical needs.

Schools need to have a written policy, reviewed annually, covering the education of pupils with medical needs. This could stand alone or be part of the SEN policy; guidance encourages schools to publish details in the school prospectus.

Pupils with long-term medical needs attending mainstream school will require at least a health care plan as recommended in *Managing Medicines in Schools and Early Years Settings*, DfES, 2005. In early years settings the plan may be informed by the Family Service Plan which is a feature of the Early Support Family Pack. The guidance points out that each pupil's individual needs should be considered when drawing up the plan in conjunction with the parents and, where appropriate, the child and child's medical carers. The plan should set out in detail the measures needed to support a pupil in school and often will need to be drawn up alongside an Individual Education Plan covering a child's special educational needs and provision.

In Wales Circular 34/97, *Supporting Pupils with Medical Needs in Schools* with its supporting good practice guide, covers similar ground.

Sick children with SEN

Sometimes parents consider that during a long illness their child has special educational needs which cannot be met by an IEP or health care plan alone. Although some pupils with medical needs may not require SEN provision, if their medical conditions prevent or hinder their access to education, then they could have learning difficulties as defined in the law and may require special educational provision.

The question is whether a child's needs are educational. If so, as with other learning difficulties, help may be provided through the model recommended by the SEN Code and described in this handbook. If the local authority decides a statutory assessment is necessary, a range of professionals who have dealings with the child will contribute advice. For pupils with mental health problems and pupils with progressive or degenerative medical conditions, *Access to Education* guidance stresses the need for a rapid response from the various agencies and professionals contributing to identification of SEN, statutory assessment and provision. It should be noted, however, that the courts have ruled that nursing care and medical attention is not educational (City of Bradford v A 1997 [ELR 1997417]).

The main disadvantage with statementing of sick children is that the procedure takes at least six months to complete and some children will be on their way to recovery before a Statement can be put into effect.

LA responsibilities for sick children

Local authorities have statutory duties in relation to providing education for children out of school because of illness. *"Each local education authority shall make arrangements for the provision of suitable education at school or otherwise than at school for those children of compulsory school age who, by reason of illness, exclusion from school or otherwise, may not for any period receive suitable education unless such arrangements are made for them."* (S19 EA96 as amended by S47 EA97)

Local authorities should ensure that pupils who are unable to attend school because of a long term or recurring medical condition have a Personal Education Plan and receive some education within 15 working days. If a child is expected to be away from school for more than 15 working days, *Access to Education* says they should receive education immediately they are absent. The guidance points out that it is the total time of predicted absence from school, rather than the time in hospital, that should be considered. Local authorities will also prepare a reintegration plan for children who have been out of school for a long period due to medical needs.

Local authorities should have a written policy statement on providing education for children and young people with medical needs who are unable to attend school. This should be available to parents and schools and should explain what they can expect from the authority and others. Each local authority should have a senior officer responsible for education of children out of school because of medical needs.

Education for children with medical needs is often provided in hospital schools or via hospital teaching services or home tuition. *Access to Education* strongly recommends a minimum entitlement of five hours teaching per week which should be increased where necessary, particularly when a pupil is approaching public exams. In the case of children with chronic fatigue syndrome or ME, the guidance accepts that some young people may be too severely affected to participate in any education. They should not be pressured to study but encouraged to resume education *"in a way which is likely to be sustainable"*.

Where the child's absence from school relates to a chronic condition, *Access to Education* says that local authorities should ensure education provision is made as soon as the child can benefit from it. Because many local authorities wait until three weeks has gone by, some children with many repeated short absences from school miss out on much needed support and slip behind at school.

'Suitable' education

A case involving a 16-year-old girl, Beth Tandy, which was decided by the House of Lords, illustrated the need for education authorities to provide suitable education. Beth had been diagnosed as suffering from ME some years earlier and became unable to attend school. The case arose when her home tuition was cut from five hours a week to three as part of an economy drive by East Sussex County Council. The Lords ruled that an authority is not entitled to take account of the availability of financial resources when deciding what sort of education is suitable. They had a statutory duty to provide education suitable to a child's age, ability and aptitude and to any special educational needs s/he may have (S19(6) EA96). The Lords accepted that if there was more than one way of providing suitable education, the council would be entitled to have regard to its resources in choosing between the different ways of providing it. But they may not reduce a statutory duty to the level of a discretionary power. (R v E. Sussex (ex parte Tandy) 1998 [ELR 1998 80])

Local authorities also have the power to provide suitable "education otherwise than at school" for young people, that is, a person over compulsory school age but under the age of 18 (S194 EA96).

Flexi-schooling and part-time education

Children may attend school part-time where they are not well enough to put in a full day. Flexible arrangements made on a regular basis, perhaps as often as week-by-week, best suit the needs of some children. Arrangements may be made for sick children to attend more than one school or be educated at school for part of the day and at home for the rest.

Dual registration (described in the **Education (Pupil Registration) Regulations 1995 SI 2089**) covers situations where two institutions have shared responsibility for the education of a pupil e.g. a child at a pupil referral unit returning to a mainstream school on a phased basis. The head of each school/unit will authorise the pupil's absence when the pupil is attending the other. Absences would also need to be authorised by the school to cover periods when the child was resting or doing work at home. The school will continue to receive funding for a child on roll at the school even if they are not well enough to attend every day but the local authority may fund home tuition for periods when the child cannot attend.

Sick children must not be taken off the school register without the consent of their parent, even after long absences for ill health, unless the school medical officer certifies them as unlikely to be in a fit state of health to attend school before ceasing to be of compulsory school age.

Hospital schools and teaching services

Hospital and other education services for children with medical problems must either be established as hospital schools, which are designated special schools, or be registered with the DfES as pupil referral units (PRUs). Provision of the National Curriculum is not obligatory in either case. *Access to Education* says that it is good practice for pupil referral units that provide for pupils with medical needs to cater exclusively for them. Most of the children being educated by hospital schools or hospital teaching services are in-patients although a few chronically ill children may attend daily from home. Some children may attend hospital school for part of the week, while spending the rest of the week being taught at home or in mainstream school.

Special schools

There are two main types of special schools:
- maintained special schools (community or foundation)
- non-maintained special schools (usually run by charities or non-profit-making bodies) approved under **S342 EA96**
plus
- independent schools which may be approved under **S347 EA96** for admission of a child with a Statement.

Maintained special schools

A programme of change for special schools was mapped out by a working group set up by the government in 2002. The group was set up in response to concern from those working in special schools who feared the government's pro-inclusion agenda might leave them without a clear role in the future. It proposed that they should increasingly cater for the growing population of children with severe and complex special educational needs; that they should be outward-looking centres of expertise and work more collaboratively with mainstream schools; and that the special school sector should go through a process of change in terms of leadership, teaching and learning, funding and structures and in the way in which they work with health, social services and other agencies which provide support beyond the classroom.

There are wide variations between local authorities in the percentage of statemented children placed in special schools. In some local authorities, disabled children are seven times more likely to be placed in a special school than others.

Children in special schools will normally have a Statement, although there are a few exceptions when, for example, children without Statements are placed in hospital special schools or are admitted to a special school following a change in circumstances or during a statutory assessment (*see page 42*).

Special schools must publish details about admission arrangements in their annual school prospectus. This should include an agreed pupil number for the whole school, rather than a particular year group. It should be borne in mind, however, that the SEN Code advises that when a local authority is considering whether to name a special school on an individual child's Statement, it considers the number in the class to which the child would be admitted, rather than the total for the whole school. Some flexibility is allowed, however, to occasionally place additional pupils at special schools. Local authorities should consult the school (and the school's local authority if it is in a different area) before naming it in a Statement.

Proposed changes in special schools

The Secretary of State and the National Assembly have issued Regulations concerning maintained special schools. They are concerned with publishing proposals for setting up, altering or closing such schools under S31 of the **School Standards and Framework Act 1998.**

Proposals must be published where a school plans to:
- increase admissions by ten per cent or more or by 20 pupils or more (or five in a school which only takes boarders) whichever is the lesser.
- change the upper or lower age limits
- change from a single-sex school to a co-educational school, or vice versa
- introduce or end boarding provision or alter provision as specified in Schedule 1
- change the type of SEN which the school provides for
- transfer the school to a new site
- in Wales, alterations to teaching in Welsh and English affecting specified numbers of pupils
- in England, any decrease in the number of pupils for whom the school normally provides.

Schedule 2 of the Regulations sets out what must be included in the published proposals; Schedule 3 describes information to be provided to the school organisation committee or Secretary of State (England) or the National Assembly (Wales).

Where the proposals are to close a maintained special school, local authorities or the governing body must publish the names of all local authorities who have children placed in the school and the numbers of such children; details of alternative provision to be made for the pupils; details of arrangements for school staff to transfer to other schools; distance and travelling times from the school to the alternative schools to which pupils may transfer and proposed travel arrangements; details of the curriculum at the alternative schools; details of any transitional arrangements in connection with the transfer of pupils to other schools, and details of any savings as a result of the proposals and a statement as to whether the school premises will be sold and the estimated proceeds of the sale.

Proposals must be published in at least one newspaper which circulates in the local authority area and must be posted at or near the main entrance to the school. Anyone may make objections to any proposals published under S31.

Education (Maintained Special Schools) (England) Regulations 1999 SI 2212; Education (Maintained Special Schools) (Wales) Regulations 1999 SI 1780.

Non-maintained special schools

These are schools in England approved by the Secretary of State under S342 of the Education Act 1996 as special schools which are not maintained by the state but charge fees on a non-profit-making basis. Most non-maintained special schools are run by major charities or charitable trusts. These schools are governed by the Education (Non-Maintained Special Schools) Regulations 1999 [SI 2257] as amended by the Education (Non-Maintained Special Schools) Regulations 2002 [SI 1982] and the Secretary of State may withdraw approval if a school fails to comply with the Regulations. Schools must publish a detailed prospectus each year which they must make available to parents.

A list of non-maintained special schools is published by the Secretary of State.

Independent schools which admit children with SEN

The arrangements for independent schools are similar to those for non-maintained special schools. To admit children with Statements they must meet a number of criteria set out in Regulations. These concern the fitness of the proprietor, having sufficient staff and adequate premises. The school must provide a written report on each statemented child to the local authority at least once a year to enable the authority to carry out a review of the Statement. This should include information about parents' involvement in any assessment or review of the child's SEN. The local authority which places a statemented child at a school must be allowed access to inspect the child and the facilities and provision available to the child. In a boarding school, the school must provide reasonable opportunities and encouragement to parents to visit a child with a Statement who is a boarder. The Secretary of State may withdraw approval from an independent school if there is a failure on the school's part to comply with any of the requirements of approval.

Transport

Local authorities have a duty to provide free school transport as they "consider necessary" to any pupil, including those below statutory school age but under sixth-form age (**S509 EA96**). The local authority must ask whether free transport is really needed to help the child to attend school. This will depend on all the circumstances such as the walking distance between home and school, the child's age, health and special needs and/or disability and any family and social circumstances. It is the responsibility of parents to ensure their child attends school unless s/he qualifies for transport provision because of particular needs or the distance s/he lives from home.

Details of who is entitled to free transport, any criteria used, and how to apply should be included in the local authority's policy on transport for children with special educational needs. The policy should have been approved by the elected members. (*See below.*)

Local authorities will normally provide free transport for any child of eight or over and of compulsory school age who lives more than three miles away from their nearest suitable school and for any child under eight who lives more than two miles away from their nearest suitable school.

Sections 509 AA–AC EA96 require local authorities to prepare a transport policy statement each year setting out what travel arrangements they consider it necessary to make for pupils of sixth form age.

Children with Statements may also receive transport help under **S324 (5)(a) EA96**. This says that unless the child's parents have made suitable arrangements, the local authority may arrange any non-educational provision specified in the Statement. This a discretionary power; local authorities need not include transport arrangements in the Statement and, even if they do, transport will generally appear in Part 6 which means the authority has no duty to provide it. The Code says local authorities should only include transport in Part 6 in exceptional cases where the child has particular transport needs.

Appropriate transport

Guidance for local authorities on transport for children with special educational needs (*Home to school transport for pupils requiring special arrangements,* DfES, 2004) recommends that the travel needs of each eligible pupil are reviewed at least annually to ensure that the provision is appropriate. It says that pupils should always travel by using mainstream arrangements and local travel schemes where they can. It recommends that local authorities undertake an assessment and management of risk in respect of each pupil entitled to travel assistance.

The guidance suggests the following forms of support are considered:

- paying for travel
- providing training for the pupil to help them travel independently
- providing a travel pass
- paying parents a mileage payment to transport their child
- providing a walking travel escort
- providing an escort to accompany a child on public transport
- providing transport from a pick-up point
- providing home to school transport.

The guidance provides advice for local authorities on providing transport for pupils with severe learning difficulties. It recommends that local authorities:

Advice for local authorities
Your statement about transport for post-16 students should address access issues for disabled students if you are to comply with the **DDA95**.

- ensure that drivers and escorts are known to parents
- maintain stable staffing over time and avoid unnecessary changes of personnel
- encourage schools and transport services to have a home-school liaison diary for each child so that parents and school staff are able to report on any issues that the other should know about.
- ensure that journey times are reasonable and that undue stress is not caused by extended periods on vehicles (*see* **Journey time** *below*).

School choice

Sometimes parents' preferred school may be further away from the child's home than another school which can meet the child's special educational needs. The local authority may name the nearer school because transport costs would not be incurred by the authority. However, it is also open to the local authority to name the school preferred by the parents on condition that the parents meet all or part of the transport costs. Clearly disagreements about whether a school is suitable for a child would be better decided by the Tribunal but in this situation parents are unable to go to Tribunal as their preferred school is already named in the Statement and Tribunals do not generally decide transport issues. The courts have said that local authorities could name two schools in a Statement to allow parents the option of appeal. Indeed in the case of R v London Borough of Havering, ex parte K (1998) [ELR 1998 402], the judge said that if a local authority only named the parent's preferred school it was not open to them to argue that a nearer school could meet the child's needs. This implies that if a local authority names the parent's preferred school, and this is over walking distance, the authority must pay transport costs unless they reach an agreement with parents that they should pay. Even then this does not commit parents to pay forever. In R v Islington Borough Council, ex parte GA (2000) [LTL 25/9/2000], changed circumstances meant the parent was no longer able to make suitable arrangements. The court said that the local authority could not fetter its discretion for all time by relying on an agreement made some years earlier.

Health and safety

The home-to-school transport guidance (*see above*) lists the safety areas where local authorities should comply with minimum service standards including:
- vehicle standards and maintenance
- on-vehicle communication
- journey times
- emergency procedures
- Criminal Record Bureau checks
- photo identification for drivers and escorts
- training for drivers and escorts
- risk assessment and management
- pupils' health needs
- monitoring and quality control.

Government guidance, *Managing Medicines in Schools and Early Years Settings*, DfES/DH, 2005, gives advice on drivers and escorts being trained as first aiders as well as being trained to deal with a medical emergency. Specific health care plans should be carried on vehicles where pupils have life threatening conditions.

Journey time

The question of the length of the school journey for children travelling to special school was raised in an important case (R v Hereford and Worcester County Council, ex parte P, 1992 [Case Law - AC0160336]). A five-year-old boy with severe learning difficulties endured a journey of an hour each way to school because of detours to pick up and drop off other children. The most direct route would have taken half an hour. The parents applied to the court for judicial review of the provision, asking that it should be extended to specify a maximum journey of 45 minutes. The court held that it was implicit that the transport which local authorities must provide under the law should be "non-stressful transport". This means that it should be such that the child reaches school without undue stress, strain or difficulty such as would prevent him benefiting from the education the school has to offer. It must also be provision which enables the child to travel in safety and in reasonable comfort. It follows from this that, where a child has a Statement, the provision of transport must be 'non-stressful'.

Transport policy

Local authorities should have a policy on transport to school covering children with SEN. This should include issues such as how entitlement is assessed and decided, criteria for assessing entitlement, arrangements for pre-school and post-16 pupils with SEN. Parents and carers should be consulted on the policy and any proposed changes. It is good practice to consult pupils too.

Other aspects which the policy should include details of:

● how family circumstances might influence a decision about free transport.

● transport arrangements for children placed at residential schools some distance from their home. Parents need to be clear about how many journeys home the authority is prepared to fund. Generally local authorities will fund parents' transport to visit residential schools before a school is named in a Statement, and periodic visits if their child becomes a pupil at a residential school. Local authorities are also advised in the Code that they should consider helping parents with travel arrangements to attend annual reviews where their child is placed outside their area.

● transport arrangements to support inclusion, for example when pupils with severe and complex special educational needs and/or disabilities attend local mainstream schools and settings for some or all of their education. The LA policy should specify arrangements for pupils with SEN registered at more than one school. The guidance points out that "*most local authorities provide travel assistance for eligible pupils at the start and end of the school day. Travel assistance during the day is often, but not always, considered to be the responsibility of schools.*"

● when the local authority would provide assistance with transport to or from extended schools.

● respite care: the guidance says that as children's services become integrated, it is reasonable to expect a corporate approach to the planning and financing of transport to respite care.

● complaints procedures.

New transport legislation and guidance

A Bill covering school transport failed to reach the statute books because of the 2005 election, but there may be plans to reintroduce the legislation. This would allow local authorities to trial new approaches to school transport. The law requiring authorities to provide free transport to most pupils where necessary would cease to be in force in pilot areas allowing authorities to charge some parents who currently receive free home-to-school transport for their children. Local authorities would have to prepare Schemes for approval by the Secretary of State to cut car use, provide for the development of localised transport schemes and improve integration and collaboration between the services provided by education, social services, health and local passenger transport services. Families on low income may be protected from charges and some safeguards for children with SEN/disabilities may also be included.

Following cases of a local authority taking into account parents' transport benefits when deciding whether transport was necessary, the DfES has clarified its 2004 guidance *Home to school transport for pupils requiring special arrangements*. Local authorities have been told: "*to avoid a potential breach of the Human Rights Act a child with mobility or other difficulties, who cannot be reasonably expected to walk to school, would have to be provided with transport or other assistance. In deciding whether transport arrangements are necessary, the local authority should look at factors such as the needs of the child, the nature of the route to school, and the suitability of existing transport options. Parental means should not play a part in the decision as to whether transport arrangements are necessary.*"

It adds: "*if a child's SEN and/or disability were such that they could not reasonably be expected to walk even relatively short distances to school, it would be unreasonable for the local authority not to provide transport.*"

Which local authority is responsible?

It may not always be clear which local authority is responsible for some groups of children, for example children of Travellers or children whose parents live abroad. The **Education (Areas to which Pupils and Students Belong) Regulations 1996 [SI 615]** describe which education authority is responsible for funding but this does not always coincide with the responsibility for providing education. If a child has special educational needs but no Statement, their support will be provided and paid for by their school, even if they are educated in the school of a different authority from where they live. In relation to assessment and statementing, it is the responsibility of the local authority where the child lives to carry out a statutory assessment and to make and maintain a Statement if necessary. That is the case even where a Statement of SEN has been made for a child in public care who is placed outside the local authority that cares for the child. However, in this case, the financial cost of the Statement will be met by the authority which cares for the child.

Government publications

Copies of Acts of Parliament and Statutory Instruments (Regulations) are available from The Stationery Office (TSO):

TSO
123 Kingsway
London WC2B 6PQ
Tel: 020 7242 6393

TSO
18-19 High Street
Cardiff CF10 1PT
Tel: 02920 39 5548
(www.tsoshop.co.uk/bookstore)

Full text of UK legislation can be downloaded free from the HMSO website:
www.opsi.gov.uk/legislation/uk.htm

Guidance issued free by the Department for Education and Skills (DfES) from:
DfES Publications
P.O. Box 5050
Annesley
Nottingham
NG15 0DL
Tel: 0845 60 222 60
Text Phone: 0845 60 555 60
Email: dfes@prolog.uk.com
www.dfespublications.gov.uk

Guidance for Wales issued free by the Welsh Assembly Government (WAG) from:
The Publications Centre
The National Assembly for Wales
Cathays Park
Cardiff
CF10 3NQ
Tel: 029 2082 3683
Fax: 029 2082 5239
www.learning.wales.gov.uk

DfES guidance

SEN Code of Practice (Ref: DfES/581/2001)
SEN Toolkit (Ref: DfES/558/2001)
Inclusive Schooling: Children with Special Educational Needs (Ref: DfES/0581/2001)
Maximising progress: ensuring the attainment of pupils with SEN [Ref: DfES/0106/2005]
Removing Barriers to Achievement, the Government's Strategy for SEN (Ref: DfES/0117/2004)
Supporting the target setting process

(revised March 2001) (Ref: DfEE 0065/2001)
Improving Behaviour and Attendance: Guidance on Exclusion from Schools and Pupil Referral Units (Ref: DfES/0354/2004)
Circular 10/99 Secretary of State's Guidance on pupil behaviour and attendance (Ref: DfES/0566/2004).
Access to Education for Children and Young People with Medical Needs (Ref: DfES/0732/2001)
Managing Medicines in Schools and Early Years Settings (1448-2005DCL-EN)
Promoting Children's Mental Health (Ref: DfEE/0112/2001)
Home to school transport for pupils requiring special arrangements (Ref: LEA0261/2004)
Special educational needs – a guide for parents and carers (Ref: DfES/0800/2001)
School Admissions (children without Statements) (Ref: DfES/0031/2003)
School Admission Appeals (children without Statements) (Ref: DfES/0030/2003)
Who does what: How social workers and carers can support the education of looked after children, 2004 [Ref: LACWDW]
Accessible Schools: Planning to increase access to schools for disabled pupils (LEA/0168/2002) and **Summary** (DfES/0462/202).

Welsh Assembly Government guidance

SEN Code of Practice for Wales, 2002
Circular 34/97, **Supporting Pupils with Medical Needs in Schools**
Handbook of Good Practice for Children with SEN, 2002
Inclusive Education, 2003 (Wales) (draft only)
Special Education Needs: information for parents and carers of children and young people who may have special educational needs, Information Document, October 2002
Circular 15/2004, **Planning to Increase Access to Schools for Disabled Pupils**
Circular 3/99, **Pupil Support and Social Inclusion** (exclusion guidance)
Circular 1/2004, **Exclusion from Schools and Pupil Referral Units** (amended by Circular 1(A) 2004)

Where to find out more

Internet resources

The Distribution of Resources to Support Inclusion (LEA 080/2001) (www.teacher net.gov.uk/docbank/index.cfm?id=5964)

National Curriculum Inclusion Statement (www.nc.uk.net/inclusion.html)

Early Support Family Pack (www.earlysupport.org.uk/pilot2/families/)

Inclusion: Providing Effective Learning Opportunities for All (www.nc.uk/net/inclusion)

Complaint about the Council? Local Government Ombudsman (see also Useful Organisations) 0845 602 1983 (www.lgo.org.uk)

Other useful publications

(contact details of publishers under Useful Organisations)

From ACE
Short Guide to the law on Equal Opportunities and Human Rights Legislation
Short Guide to the SEN and Disability Act 2001
Children with SEN – Sources of Help
Taking Matters Further
Home School Transport
The Warnock Summary
My Child in School advice booklets:
Early Years Extra Help
Getting Extra Help
Asking for a Statutory Assessment
Getting the Statement Right
Understanding Annual Reviews
Disability Discrimination
Making a Complaint
Permanent Exclusion
Fixed Period Exclusion
Tackling Bullying
Choosing a School
Appealing for a School
Websites that Work for Parents, 2004, guide to parent-friendly websites aimed at LEAs
SEN: Support for Governors, 2003, training materials for governing bodies
The IPS Pack, 2005, ACE/CDC training materials for independent parental supporters and those advising parents on SEN.
Governors' Briefing on SEN
Children out of School, 2003.

From SENDIST
How to Appeal
Right to be Heard (video)
How to Make a Claim
Answering a claim of disability discrimination – a guide for responsible bodies, 2002

From the Disability Rights Commission
The Code of Practice for Schools on the Disability Discrimination Act 1995: Part 4, 2002
How do I make a claim? A guide to taking a Part 4 Schools DDA case
A guide for parents
The Disability Discrimination Act Part 4 – A governor's guide

From Estyn
Best practice in the development of Statements of special educational needs and delivery by schools of the action agreed, 2004

From Ofsted
SEN and disability: towards inclusive schools, 2004
Inclusion: the impact of LA support and outreach services, 2005

From ACCAC
Statutory Assessment and Reporting Arrangements (for each key stage)
A focus on achievement – guidance on including pupils with additional needs in whole school target setting, 2001, (Ref: AC/GM/0229) ISBN: 1 86112 397 3 ACCAC Publications, PO Box 9B, Thames Ditton, Surrey KT8 0BN

From the QCA
Assessment and Reporting Arrangements (for each key stage)
Changes to the key stage 4 curriculum, QCA 2003
Disapplication of the National Curriculum (Circular 0118/2000)
Modern foreign languages in the key stage 4 curriculum, 2004
Work-related learning for all at key stage 4, 2003

From other government departments
Every Child Matters, 2003 (www.everychildmatters.gov.uk/publications) Also available from The Stationery Office, address above.

Framework for the Assessment of Children in Need and their Families jointly issued by the Department of Health, the Department for Education and Employment and the Home Office, 2000.

From legal publishers
The Law of Education, loose leaf manual published by Butterworths LexisNexis (www.butterworths.com)

Education Law Reports, case law published by Jordans (www.jordanpublishing.co.uk)

From SEN publishers
Special Education Directory, 2005, special schools directory published by the School Government Publishing Company, Darby House, Redhill, Surrey, RH1 3DN
Tel: 01737 642223
(www.schoolgovernment.co.uk)

Schools for Special Needs 2005-6, published by Gabbitas, Carrington House, 126-130 Regent Street, London W1B 5EE
Tel: 020 7734 0161
(www.gabbitas.co.uk)

Making it Work, training pack for schools and LEAs on disability discrimination, published by Council for Disabled Children and Disability Equality in Education

Useful organisations
Statutory organisations and quangos
Department for Education and Skills (DfES)
Sanctuary Buildings
Great Smith Street
London SW1P 3BT
Tel: 020 7925 5000 (www.dfes.gov.uk)

National Assembly for Wales
Cardiff Bay
Cardiff
CF99 1NA
Tel: 02920 825111 (www.wales.gov.uk)

Council on Tribunals
81 Chancery Lane
London WC2A 1BQ
Tel: 020 7855 5200
(www.council-on-tribunals.gov.uk)

Commissioner for Local Administration in England (Local Government Ombudsman)
Adviceline: 0845 602 1983 (open between 9.00am and 4.30pm Monday to Friday) (www.lgo.org.uk)
There are three areas which deal with complaints from different parts of the country.

Complaints from London boroughs north of the river Thames (including Richmond but not including Harrow or Tower Hamlets), Essex, Kent, Surrey, Suffolk, East and West Sussex, Berkshire, Buckinghamshire, Hertfordshire and the City of Coventry
10th Floor
Millbank Tower
Millbank
London SW1P 4QP
Tel: 020 7217 4620

London Borough of Tower Hamlets, City of Birmingham, Solihull MBC, Cheshire, Derbyshire, Nottinghamshire, Lincolnshire and the north of England (except the Cities of York and Lancaster)
Beverley House
17 Shipton Road
York YO30 5FZ
Tel: 01904 380200

London boroughs south of the river Thames (except Richmond) and Harrow; the Cities of York and Lancaster; and the rest of England, not included in the above
The Oaks No 2
Westwood Way
Westwood Business Park
Coventry CV4 8JB
Tel: 024 7682 0000

Information Commissioner
Enforces and oversees Data Protection Act 1998 and Freedom of Information Act 2000
Information Commissioner
Wycliffe House
Water Lane
Wilmslow
Cheshire SK9 5AF
(www.informationcommissioner.gov.uk)
Learning and Skills Council
Cheylesmore House
Quinton Road
Coventry
CV1 2WT
Tel: 0845 019 4170; General enquiries: 0870 900 6800; (www. lsc.gov.uk)

Special Educational Needs and Disability Tribunal
(www.sendist.gov.uk)

Address for SEN Appeals
SENDIST
Ground floor
Mowden Hall
Staindrop Road
Darlington
DL3 9BG
SEN helpline: 0870 241 2555

Address for disability claims
SENDIST
Procession House
55 Ludgate Hill
London
EC4M 7JW
Disability helpline: 0870 606 5750

Office for Standards in Education
Ofsted
Alexandra House
33 Kingsway
London WC2B 6SE
www.ofsted.gov.uk
Inspects schools and local education
authorities in England.

Inspectorate for Education and Training in Wales (Estyn)
Anchor Court
Keen Road
Cardiff
CF24 5JW
Tel: 029 2044 6446 (www.estyn.gov.uk)
Inspects schools and local education
authorities in Wales.

Qualifications and Curriculum Authority
83 Piccadilly
London
W1J 8QA
Tel: 020 7509 5555; Enquiry line: 020
7509 5556; Minicom: 020 7509 6546
(www.qca.org.uk)

Sources of information and advice
Advisory Centre for Education
1C Aberdeen Studios
22 Highbury Grove
London N5 2DQ
Tel: 0207 704 3370 (business)
0808 8005793 (general advice);
0808 8000 327 (exclusion advice);

0207 704 9822 (free exclusion advice
pack) (www.ace-ed.org.uk)
Advice, training and publications for
parents and professionals.

Centre for Studies on Inclusive Education (CSIE)
New Redland
Frenchay Campus
Coldharbour Lane
Bristol, BS16 1QU
Tel: 0117 328 4007
(www. inclusion.uwe.ac.uk/csie)
Publishes Index for Inclusion (one version
for schools and one for early years).

Independent Panel for Special Education Advice (IPSEA)
6 Carlow Mews
Woodbridge
Suffolk IP12 1EA
Advice line: 0800 0184016; Tribunal
appeals only: 01394 384711; General
enquiries: 01394 380518
(www.ipsea.org.uk)
Offers free telephone advice for parents of
children with special educational needs.
Refers children for a free second professional opinion where appropriate and provides free advice and representation where
appropriate for parents appealing to the
SENDIST. Supports parents in preparing
their appeal to the SENDIST.

Contact a Family
209-211 City Road, London EC1V 1JN
Tel: 020 7608 8700; Helpline 0808 808
3555 or Textphone 0808 808 3556
(www.cafamily.org.uk)
Has links with a substantial number of
independent self-help/support groups and
contacts throughout the country with an
emphasis on children and young people.
Helpline offers information and support
when a child has been diagnosed with a
specific disabling condition or rare disorder.

Contact a Family Wales
Contact a Family Cymru
Room 153 S
1st Floor
The Exchange Building
Mount Stuart Square
Cardiff CF10 5EB
Tel: 029 2049 8001
(www.cafamily.org.uk/wales)

Education Otherwise
PO Box 7420
London N9 9SG
Advice: 0870 7300074
(www. education-otherwise.org)
Self-help organisation for parents educating their children at home.

Home Education Advisory Service (HEAS)
P.O. Box 98
Welwyn Garden City
Herts
AL8 6AN
Phone/Fax: (01707 371854
(www.heas.org.uk)
Information, advice and support for home educating families in England and Wales.

Network 81
1-7 Woodfield Terrace
Stansted
Esssex
CM24 8AJ
Helpline: 0870 770 3306;
(www.network81.co.uk)
National network of parents working for properly resourced inclusive education.

Parents for Inclusion
Unit 2
70 South Lambeth Road
London SW8 1RL
Advice line: 0800 652 3145
(www.parentsforinclusion.org)
Helps parents of children with SEN to get support for their children in mainstream schools.

Rathbone CI
Churchgate House
56 Oxford Street
Manchester M1 6EU
Advice Line: 0800 917 6790
(www.literacytrust.org.uk)
Provides advice and support to professionals and parents of children with SEN.

National Bureau for Students with Disabilities (SKILL)
Skill, Chapter House, 18-20 Crucifix Lane, London SE1 3JW. Tel: 020 7450 0620
(www.skill.org.uk)
Aims to develop opportunities for young people and adults with learning difficulties in further, higher and adult education, in training and the transition to employment.

Legal advice
Bar Pro Bono Unit
289-293 High Holborn
6th Floor
London
WC1V 7HZ
Tel: 020 7611 9500 (answerphone)
(www.barprobono.org.uk)
Provides free legal advice and representation in certain cases where public funding is not available or where the applicant is unable to afford legal assistance. Advice, representation and assistance with mediation is provided by a panel of barristers.

Children's Legal Centre
University of Essex
Wivenhoe Park
Colchester
Essex CO4 3SQ
Advice line: 0845 456 6811
(www.childrenslegalcentre.com)
Independent national charity concerned with law and policy affecting children and young people. The Education Law and Advocacy Unit provides parents with comprehensive legal advice for those in conflict with schools and/or local authorities.

Community Legal Service Direct
Tel:0845 435 4 435 (www.clsdirect.org.uk)
Referral to legal help and representation via the CLS directory of specialist advisers and lawyers.

Education Law Association
ELAS
33, College Road,
Reading. RG6 1QE.
Tel: 01189 669866
(www.educationlawassociation.org.uk)
The association has lists of members who are lawyers, educational psychologists, advice workers etc, some of whom will accept referrals.

The Law Centres Federation
Duchess House,
18-19 Warren Street,
London W1T 5LR
Tel 020 7387 8570
(www.lawcentres.org.uk)
Provides an initial point of contact for those seeking information and advice, both within the movement, outside agencies and to the general public.

Law Society solicitors online service
(www.lawsociety.org.uk/
choosingandusing/findasolicitor.law)
Information on solicitors – specialisms, languages, location, website links.

Professional Organisations
**Association of Workers for Children with
Emotional and Behavioural Difficulties**
AWCEBD, Charlton Court
East Sutton
Maidstone
Kent ME17 3DQ
Tel: 01611 843104 (www.sebda.org)
Promotes excellence in services for chil-
dren and young people who have emotion-
al and behavioural difficulties and to sup-
port those who work with them.

The British Psychological Society
St Andrews House
48 Princess Road East
Leicester LE1 7DR
Tel: 0116 254 9568 (www.bps.org.uk)
The BPS cannot refer parents to an individual psychologist but its register of chartered psychologists, which may be available at large reference libraries, lists its
members who must abide by the Society's
Code of Conduct. Among the services
offered by chartered psychologists are
clinical psychology, counseling psychology
and educational psychology.

Chartered Society of Physiotherapy
14 Bedford Row
London WC1R 4ED
020 7306 6666; (www.csp.org.uk)

College of Occupational Therapists
106 – 114 Borough High Street
Southwark
London SE1 1LB
Tel: 020 7357 6480 (www.cot.co.uk)

Royal College of Speech and Language
Therapists
2 White Hart Yard
London SE1 1NX
Tel: 020 7378 1200 (www.rcslt.org)

**National Association for Special
Educational Needs (NASEN)**
NASEN House
4/5 Amber Business Village

Amber Close
Amington
Tamworth
Staffordshire
B77 4RP
Tel: 01827 311500 (www.nasen.org.uk)
Promotes the development of children with
SEN and supports professionals who work
with them.

Special needs computer advice
Aiding Communication in Education (ACE)
The ACE Centre and ACE North provide a
focus for the use of technology to support
the communication and educational needs
of young people with physical and communication difficulties.
The ACE Centre
92 Windmill Road
Oxford OX3 7DR
Tel: 01865 759 800

ACE North, Units 11 & 12 Gatehead
Business Park, Delph, Saddleworth OL3
5DE. Tel: 01457 829444
(www.ace-centre.org.uk)
Information, support and training with technology for people with communication difficulties.

Advisory Unit Computers in Education
126 Great North Road
Hatfield
Hertfordshire AL9 5JZ
Tel: 01707 266 714 (www.advisory-
unit.org.uk)
Offers ICT services and educational soft-
ware to schools. AUCE has expertise in the
use of IT to support pupils who have
severe learning difficulties, moderate
learning disabilities and specific learning
difficulties.

Disability organisations
Council for Disabled Children
CDC
National Children's Bureau
8 Wakely Street
London EC1V 7QE
Tel: 020 7843 6058 (www. ncb.org.uk/cdc)
Promotes collaborative work and partner-
ship between different organisations pro-
viding services and support for children
with disabilities and SEN.

Disability Law Service
39-45 Cavell Street
London E1 2BP
Tel: 020 7791 9800
(www.city.ac.uk/icsl/current_students/pro_
bono/disability_ls.html)
Provides up-to-date, informed legal advice
for people with disabilities, their families,
enablers and carers and undertakes case-
work representing disabled people at every
stage of the legal process. Areas of law
covered: employment, disability discrimination; welfare rights; community care;
education; consumer and contract.

Disability Rights Commission
FREEPOST
MID 02164
Stratford upon Avon
CV37 9BR
DRC Helpline: 08457 622 633; Textphone
08457 622 644; (www.drc-gb.org)

**Royal Association for Disability and
Rehabilitation (RADAR)**
RADAR
12 City Forum
250 City Road
London EC1V 8AF
Tel: 020 7250 3222 (www.radar.org.uk)
RADAR is a campaigning organisation run
by disabled people and working to remove
barriers that restrict disabled people's daily
lives. It works alongside 400 national and
local organisations around the UK that
make up their membership.

Index

health
    access of children with medical
        needs to mainstream 120
    advice for statutory assessment
        12, 30, 38, 40, 41
    and special educational needs 36
    children ill at home 119-120
    health authority duties to children
        with SEN 10, 12
    health authority duty to have
        regard to the Code 8
    health care plan 37, 118
    hospital schools and services 119,
        120
    medical advice 30, 41, 118
    mental health 118
    Personal Education Plan 119
    provision in Statement 63
    pupil referral unit 120
    therapy 49
home education
    attendance proceedings 57
    LA responsibilities 56
    removing child from school roll
        57
    statemented child at home 56-57,
        68
home tuition 119
hospital schools and education
    services 119, 120
Human Rights Act 1998 56 89, 118

inclusion
    accessibility plans 97-98, 103
    accessibility strategies 97
    admission conditions 50
    duty to educate in mainstream
        50-52, 61
    exclusion of pupils with SEN
        110-111
    National Curriculum inclusion
        statement 23
Independent Panel for Special Educ-
    ation Advice (IPSEA) 40, 85, 130
independent parental supporter 33,
    58, 60
independent schools
    approval 54, 122
    disagreement resolution 77

independent schools *continued*
    parents making representations
        for 54-55
    pupils paid for by authority 113
    type of school 18
Individual Education Plan (IEP)
    child involvement 22
    devising and recording 22, 47
    group education plan 23
    review of 22, 23
information
    agencies sharing 16
    Commissioner 114, 115
    complaints 114,115
    for parents 14, 15, 20, 35, 114-115
    for disabled pupils 98
    interpreters and translators 44, 60,
        76, 116
    school choice, information 51, 60,
        103
    school records 114-115
    school information requirements
        14-15
inspection
    accessibility plan 98
    accessibility strategy 97
    disability conciliation service 78
    Every Child Matters agenda 16
    new arrangements 16
    school choice 60

Key stage 4 pupils 72, 104-105

language
    home language different, not a
        learning difficulty 7, 115
    interpreters and translators 44, 60,
        76, 116
    jargon 3
Learning and Skills Act 2000 17
learning difficulties
    criteria for assessment 35-36
    definition 7
legal action
    appeals Tribunal 78-89
    High Court appeal 88-89, 99
    judicial review 89
    negligence 90

ACE advice

ACE's freephone helpline service includes four advice lines run each afternoon between 2 and 4 pm. Two lines are dedicated to parents whose children have been excluded from school and two lines cover a range of issues including special educational needs, bullying, admissions and attendance. In addition we run morning and afternoon advice lines for callers referred to us through the Parentline advice service. We also run special lines for advisers trained in the use of our education manual as part of our Step-by-Step advice package.

ACE General line
0808 800 5793

ACE Exclusion line
0808 8000 327

ACE information line (callers requiring an exclusion information pack should leave their name and address on this line)
020 7704 9822

ACE website: www.ace-ed.org.uk
Online support for parents who are having difficulty with their children's education.

ACE website links you to our publications list , enables you to order and download publications, access our free exclusion pack and read the answers to FAQs on line.

ACE advice service relies on donations, grants and income from publication sales and training fees. You can make a donation via our website. If your company or workplace supports charities, consider making ACE your charity of the year. Contact ACE for posters and leaflets.

ACE advice publications

ACE's My Child in School booklets form the backbone of our advice publications for parents. They explain step-by-step what to do if you are choosing a school, appealing for a school place, asking for extra help for your child, getting a Statement for your child, or making a complaint. They cover the following topics but the list continues to expand, so phone our advice line if your problem is not covered here:

Choosing a School
Appealing for a School
Tackling Bullying
Getting Extra Help
Early Years Extra Help
Asking for a Statutory Assessment
Getting the Statement Right
Understanding Annual Reviews
Disability Discrimination
Making a Complaint
School Attendance
Fixed Period Exclusion
Permanent Exclusion

Send a cheque or PO for £1.60 with a stamped addressed envelope for any booklet.

ACE publications for parents also cover other topics. They include:
Special Educational Needs: sources of help
(over 100 addresses of useful organisations)
Taking Matters Further (comprehensive information on complaints)
Home Education (parents' rights and responsibilities if they choose to educate their child at home)
All the above £2.50 including postage

Children Out of School, a guide to the law on education of children in pupil referral units, children with health problems, home education, attendance issues and exclusion £12 plus £2 p&p

For a free publications list, phone or send a sae to **ACE, 1C Aberdeen Studios, 22 Highbury Grove, London N5 2DQ.**
Full list also on our website: **www.ace–ed.org.uk**